WEALTH BUILDING METHODS FOR YOU:
To Make Your Dreams Come True

Dr. AC Brown

Using the

P.A.U.S.E.

(Practical Application and Use of the Scriptures Everyday)

Wealth **B**uilding **S**ystem

Empowering You Spiritually and Abundantly with
How to Unlock the Promises of God in Your Life
No Matter What You Do for a Living

"All the kings of the earth shall praise thee, O LORD, when
they hear the words of thy mouth."

Psalm 138:4

Doing It God's Way®

WHAT PEOPLE ARE SAYING ABOUT THIS BOOK

Hello my friend, and to whom it may concern. It is indeed an honor and a pleasure to be able to voice my opinion as it relates to this fantastic, easy-reading, life-giving, abundant money-earning book that I have just finished reading from cover to cover. I mean, I picked it up, and could hardly put it down. I am both happy and humbled beyond measure to be able to share with you, Dr. Brown, just how much I have admired and bragged on you over the years. I tell people all the time, Dr. Brown might not be the best in the world at sowing service and harvesting money; but he would do it until the best comes long. His uncanny ability keeps you studying, laughing, helping God's people, and making money. Dr. Brown, you are a family man too, aren't you? By the way, if any of you want to know how to get married and stay married, you better be sure to talk to Dr. AC Brown and Gladys Brown. Gladys Brown is one of the prettiest little ladies (mind, body, and soul) I have ever seen in my life.

It is evidenced subliminally that AC and Gladys (after celebrating their 60th wedding anniversary of happy, blissful marriage); that a good marriage is the beginning of success in life. Young men and women, after you get a good education; if you will put a real marriage and family on your list, God will bless you beyond measure.

I must stop now, as you can see, I can go on and on writing about my long-term friend Dr. AC Brown. I want to close by saying, if you will read this book over and over again, you will learn to study to show yourself approved, work hard, and smart. You will know without a doubt, how to learn and have a burning desire to help God's people live a fuller and better life. You will be able to sow excellence in service to God's people and believe me my friend, God will overpay you (money) for your love and commitment to His Divine Cause.

Dr. Brown, you have outdone yourself this time. You have combined the best selling techniques known to man and undergirded them with the Words of God and the teachings of Jesus Christ. Other than the Word of God and the teachings of Christ, this is the best book on helping God's people and making an abundance of money while doing it, I have ever read.

May God continue to smile on you and yours. We love you.

Pastor Ron Brown
Peach real estate Inc.

୨୦   ୯୨

Let me introduce myself. My name is Brenda Smith. I am a Sales Representative in Real Estate. I have been in business for seven years. I met Dr. AC Brown in 2004; the day I met Dr. Brown I knew right then, he was a child of God.

Dr. Brown would always tell me, *"If you want to be successful, you have to do it God's way."* I listened and sold over five million dollars in sales. I would always listen to Dr. Brown; his message was very powerful.

This book has inspired me by the Holy Spirit and the sweet Grace of God. It feels good to know that the Lord has worked with me at my time of need. Now my life can begin. For so long, I felt dead and alone, not really knowing where I stood in life, but I have found that I am special to my Father.

I am not an extraordinary human being, but I am someone in God. I hope that each and every reader, young and mature, will find that inner peace with our Lord, our God. I pray that after sharing my experiences about my life in God, your hearts and spirits will receive any message that the Lord is trying to give to you.

Brenda Smith
Real estate sales Representative

Wealth Building Methods For YOU:

To Make Your Dreams Come True

Using the
P.A.U.S.E. ®
(Practical Application and Use of the Scriptures Everyday)
Wealth Building System

Doing It God's Way®

Dr. AC Brown
BS, MM, DD

Published by:

eBlessings.us
P. O. Box 601
Stone Mountain, GA 30086
www.info@eblessings.us; eblessings@gmail.com
www.acbrown@eblessings.us

Wealth Building Methods: To Make Your Dreams Come True"
Using the P.A.U.S.E.®: Practical Application and Use of Scriptures
Everyday Wealth Building System

For further information, you may write to above address or:

Alonza C. Brown
5533 Silver Ridge Drive
Stone Mountain, Georgia 30087

Scripture quotations from the Holy Bible, King James Version unless
otherwise specified.

ISBN: 1453715487
EAN-13: 9781453715482

Printed by eBlessings
Atlanta, Georgia
Layout, design, editing, composition, writing and cover design by:
James Anthony Allen, eBlessings.us, Atlanta, Georgia

Alonza C. Brown's books and books from the eBlessings' Network
are available at special quantity discounts for bulk purchases for
sales promotions, premiums, fund-raising, or educational use.

Special books or book excerpts can also be created to fit specific
needs. For details, write: Special Marketing, eBlessings, P.O. Box
601, Stone Mountain, GA 30086.

DEDICATION

This book is gratefully dedicated to

<u>My wife:</u>

Gladys L. Brown

<u>My two sons:</u>

Alonza C. Brown Jr.

Reginald M. Brown

and

All men, women, boys, and girls

Who want to succeed in life

by

Doing It God's Way®

CONTENTS

Contents

Contents

ACKNOWLEDGEMENTS

What I gave up for Father God to put together this book series and the enterprises to follow: a) two hundred and thirty-five houses, most of them free and clear, mostly single-family homes collecting $800-$900 a month in rental fees; b) a $350,000 annual income for many years selling single-family homes. This was my personal sales income not the sales income of a sales team. I was using the *Pathway to Success* and applying the Scriptures daily in my life, "Doing it God's Way".

Before all that, I worked nine hours a night putting myself through college. My daddy was a rich man; he wanted to send me to college. However, I remembered right off what the Scripture says, *"Acknowledge Him and He will direct your paths."* The Lord spoke saying, *"Work your way through college and leave your daddy the money."* It is not too late for you to start operating this way. God sees and hears everything. That is when my success started.

I have built, rented, owned, and sold single-family homes, sub-divisions, and apartment home communities. I am 81 years of age and can get up stairs better than many fifty year olds can. I can see and hear better than most people my age. This should have your attention. If I had another 48 years to travel this earth, I don't know what I would do differently. If I travel this earth another 48 years, I would have other records of accomplishment to share with you. Use what I share with you in this book and you will have success beyond your imagination. Live life "Doing it God's Way"!

PREFACE

I go on no job, I join no church, and I do not make any major decisions before first consulting Father God, Christ Jesus, or the Holy Spirit. This is the way I have operated for a period of 48 years.

I highly recommend that you operate this way regardless of what you do for a living. Do not allow anyone to tell you not to consult Father God. He has the time and He is just that big; able to handle all of our questions. I'm not talking about asking your pastor all of those questions; but your Heavenly Father—because God is a good God and He is a very jealous God—He has the answers.

Whenever I attend church and the pastor is delivering the sermon, I stand tall praising God. I highly recommend you operate this way. The 24th Psalm which says, God and His Son Jesus owns it all; without Them, you and I cannot do anything, nor get anything worth getting on this earth.

Let me take it a step further. When I join a church, I do not leave there until or unless the Holy Spirit tells me to leave. I don't do anything on my own without asking the LORD and I advise you not to do it on your own either. The Holy Spirit has taught me this way for a period of 48 years and it is the Holy Spirit Who is bringing this program to you. The Holy Spirit is our Teacher. I challenge you to try using the Holy Spirit.

I have used what Sam Brown and the Holy Spirit has taught me during my 48-year track record on several prominent people and special events with unheralded success. Do not let life pass you by without taking a serious look at this opportunity for your personal financial and spiritual success through the P.A.U.S.E. ® Wealth Building System. If I can do it, so can you.

HOW TO USE THE P.A.U.S.E. WEALTH BUILDING SYSTEM

Let me introduce you to the P.A.U.S.E.®: Practical Application and Use of Scriptures Everyday, Wealth Building System and how to use this book and the system.

Each book in the Wealth Building series is designed using stories, anecdotes, and biographical information summarizing Alonza C. Brown's life wherein he earned nearly one million dollars three times. Found within the pages of each chapter are the scriptures which he applied throughout his life and the situations to which he applied them. They are underlined within each chapter along with key wealth building tips.

There is a summary of key "Wealth Building Scriptures" and "Wealth Building Tips" found at the end of each chapter. The "Wealth Building Scriptures" chapter summary is entitled "My Daily Commitment." The "Wealth Building Tips" chapter summary is entitled "My Daily Affirmations."

There is one scripture and tip for each day of the week. Number one, you apply Sunday, number two, you apply Monday, and number three, you apply Tuesday; and so forth. You read these scriptures aloud three times a day; good times are at meal times and at bedtime; or do it in one sitting. One time for the Father, one time for His Son, and one time for the Holy Spirit. This helps you to have the strength to do God's Will in executing today's assignments.

Each chapter represents a week, i.e., chapter one equals week one. You will notice that the chapter summaries are noted as "Week One, Week Two, Week Three," and so forth.

There are sixteen chapters in this book. This correlates to sixteen weeks. This is a sixteen-week program where success is guaranteed.

This book can be used in your personal home study, your weekly Bible study, or in any weekly or scheduled class which seeks to spiritually and economically empower its participants. This is an individual or group--daily, weekly, or sixteen-week program depending on how you want to use it. Use it to compliment your current spiritual development delivery module.

In summary, the P.A.U.S.E. Wealth Building System: Practical Application and Use of Scriptures Everyday is designed based on the life of Alonza C. Brown. He is a three-time millionaire, at one time one of the richest African-Americans living in Metro Atlanta, who is imparting into you his secrets of success. This wealth-building program has the Pathway to Success, seven cornerstone "Wealth Building Scriptures" and a plethora of "Wealth Building Tips" and information which when applied is guaranteed to bring success. These are underlined throughout each chapter.

As you start each and every day, do the *Pathway to Success.* Also, read aloud both "Daily Affirmations" and "Daily Commitments" three times a day during a 24-hour period. Do this every day with each chapter and for a period of sixteen weeks. In seminars, have the participants match the underlined words with the Wealth Building Scriptures and Tips. Life will take on a new meaning! Do it because it works!

INTRODUCTION

My name is Brother James Anthony Allen, Holy Ghost-filled Evangelist and Director of eBlessings.us, an international Internet inter-denominational social services ministry who has contributed with help from the Holy Spirit to this effort by Alonza C. Brown. In this collaboration, the LORD and His Holy Family has revealed to me what has been shared with AC over the years and is now in a form which is more palatable to the average person and can be easily understood, absorbed and thus utilized and integrated into one's daily routines.

Many of you may know AC from his Real Estate days when "white flight" was beginning and at its paramount in Atlanta, Georgia. Many people benefited from his "Jacob-like" sales techniques and others may have found him to be distasteful; but you got to love him. According to AC, all his life he always had an interest in serving people and that is why the LORD blessed him with so much material gain. You can find people on both sides of this argument. What I can say is this—AC is an elderly man looking in the face of Eternity. This has a way of motivating a person to try to do that which is good in the sight of the LORD. The fear of the Lord is the beginning of knowledge and wisdom. J. Douglas Edwards says, "The only way to motivate a man is to frighten the hell out of him."

Before AC came to our home, the Holy Spirit said to me, "AC Brown is coming over." I thought and asked my wife, "Who is AC Brown? Do you know him? Is he that old guy standing up praising God all the time at church?" Yes, that was him—AC Brown. During my life, the Holy Spirit may have told me only three times that someone was coming—this was one of those times. I knew something special was going to happen with this visit—P.A.U.S.E.® was revealed to me after four (4) years of working with AC; four tough long-suffering years.

When AC first came to the door he said, "The LORD told me to come by here." I said, "The Lord told me that you were coming." He said, "The LORD said if you do not come to the front door, go to the back door. If you and Allen have a falling out (and there were many—but the Holy Spirit directed me to keep working with him) go to the back door and keep knocking." AC also told me this. He said, "Allen, I have been a millionaire three times. Each time the LORD told me to stick with a specific person and I would make millions. Allen," he said, "this time the LORD told me to 'Stick with Allen,' and I am going to do just that. We are on our way to make millions. Allen, money will be falling like snowflakes falling from the sky in the wintertime!"

Alonza C. Brown was at one time the richest black man in Atlanta, Georgia or one of the richest. He owned and rented single-family homes and sub-divisions; and built and owned apartment home communities. He gained fortunes and lost fortunes. If you ask him how he gained his fortunes he will say from his experiences over the years but specifically what the Holy Spirit told him to do every step of the way. If you ask him how he lost his fortunes, he will say it was from business deals, jealous peers, legal fees, and attempts to launch seminars around the nation to teach people the sales techniques, which took him to the top of his field.

AC is in his eighties and is <u>imparting</u> his sales techniques and how to allow the Holy Spirit to direct your every step in an attempt to help the homeless, bring the nation out of its economic slump, give families a way to "fish" instead of receiving handouts, give people an opportunity to learn how to make a livelihood selling something (because we all are always selling something), and to make his fourth fortune before he goes on to be with our Heavenly Father.

This is what you must know about Alonza C. Brown. His family has a Real Estate company, which is highly successful.

According to AC, it is because they are using many of the principles he taught them outright or they learned surreptitiously or because of their own professionalism. They also had to sit under his playing sales audiotapes and motivational audiotapes day after day and year after year for over twenty (20) years. This technique is called repetition and is a power, which Father God has made available for us all.

It is only one of the many tools, which AC has culled over the years—from his own experiences, from those of others, from pastors and the Bible, wherein he learned to apply biblical tools (Scriptures) to his personal and business goals. Note that AC and his family goes to the top seminars around the nation—learning from the top people in the nation and around the world who teach anything and everything about selling and all there is to sell. AC is bringing to you what he has learned from these seminars, workshops and from visiting multiple churches during his forty-eight (48) year track record of selling and attempting to teach people to sell. He will tell you in a minute, "If you don't try anything, you will surely fail. You gotta try something to see if it will work for you."

AC says, "Everyone is selling something all the time. When they open their mouths they are selling something. They need to sell Father God and His Son Jesus; and they need to learn to sell something to feed themselves and their families." Therefore, AC is selling you this book, which is filled with ways for you to do just that—feed yourself and your family using God-given Scriptures which are guaranteed to give you the financial success and security which you seek or should be seeking. Enjoy reading this book as Alonza C. Brown imparts his wisdom to you.

Wealth Building Methods For YOU:

To Make Your Dreams Come True

Dr. AC Brown

Using the
P.A.U.S.E. ®
(Practical Application and Use of the Scriptures Everyday)
Wealth Building System

Doing It God's Way®

In Collaboration with
James Anthony Allen
Director, eBlessings

Chapter 1

Alonza C. Brown

Using the
P.A.U.S.E. ®
(Practical Application and Use of the Scriptures Everyday)
Wealth Building System

"For I tell you, that many prophets and kings have desired to see those things which ye see, and have not seen *them*; and to hear those things which ye hear, and have not heard *them*."

Luke 10:24

Doing It God's Way®

Chapter 1

Alonza C. Brown

A Quick Glimpse into
My 48-Year Track Record

For **48 years** I've heard people make statements like this. "If I had the proper education." Or "If I was not born with the color of this skin, I could succeed in life." "If I were only thinner... smarter... or prettier." But early in my life <u>I learned how to join forces and team up with my brothers and sisters to form a partnership for success.</u> I will teach the people across this land how I was able to do it. This wealth-building system will help many people. I have done it this way for over forty-eight (48) years. If I can do it this way, you can too.

My success started my senior year in high school. In high school I was labeled just a good old school bus driver. The principal of the high school was excited about having a speaking contest before you could graduate. He brought the Caucasian teachers from the Caucasian school to judge this contest. This was unusual.

I never had an opportunity to practice with my classmates before the speaking contest, because I drove a school bus during that class period. On the day of the contest, the judge stood and said, "Ladies and gentlemen, we have heard some good speakers today, but I'm going to have to give Alonza C. Brown first place."

Remember this always, in high school I was labeled "just a good old school bus driver." But before I left that stage that day as the good old school bus driver that I was, I made up my mind that very day that everything I would touch in life from this point forward would turn to gold.

Remember what I said – I was in high school driving a school bus to make extra money. If I can do it this way, you can too. And it is not too late to make that decision to start—to make a change in your life. Why did I make this decision? How could I make this decision? I decided I was going to use the same technique I used to win that speaking contest. If you can do it the way I did it, you're on your way to receive the real Promises of God.

The question is: How did I win that speaking contest? My sister-in-law Ruth Brown, a real-life saint, taught me at home

26

at night by the mirror. In one of Ruth Brown's training sessions, my sister-in-law said to me, "Alonza, if you want to win that speaking contest, you need to consult your daddy Sam Brown."

This is what is going on all over this land. People are sitting in churches receiving new sermons, new messages. Pastors are bringing new messages to their congregations. Motivational speakers are bringing new ideas to their audiences. The problem is—most people are sitting there, taking notes, but still doing it the same old way when they go home. They are living life the same old way, at the same old time; many not realizing it while others attempt to change but poor rooting gets in their way.

Writing it down, listening to the CD once, going home, getting out of the car and continuing doing it their same old ways. Watching and waiting for the same old shows. Eating the same old food, at the same old places. Not going anywhere. Not doing anything with their lives. Just watching television while sitting on that couch or recliner. Talking to the same old friends, about the same old stuff. God is tired of this program—the way many of you are doing it. Use this book to <u>learn to make a decision which will change your life</u> and the lives of your families by beginning to live life using the Scriptures everyday to guarantee your success—to get you out of that rut. Why do you think Father God gave you the Scriptures anyway? So you would <u>apply them to your daily</u>

living, with Divine Goals for His Divine Purposes—for His Kingdom.

Mr. Sam Brown

I **want you** to understand that Father God changed my gears that morning through Ruth Brown. When that gear shifts -- we begin to go in another direction. I'm here to testify to you that when that gear shifts, God is changing the direction that He wants you to travel. Listen at what Ruth Brown said to me.

"Alonza, if you want to win that speaking contest, you need to observe your daddy Sam Brown."

That was all she said, but that was a mouthful.

I have practiced for 48 years, disciplining myself to keep my mind on God at all times. When that gear in life shifts, I know exactly what to do. And He tells us so clearly in the Bible, If you fear Me, I'll give you riches and honor and life.

"The secret of the LORD *is* with them that fear him; and he will shew them his covenant."   Psalm 25:14 (KJV)

"O fear the LORD, ye his saints: for *there is* no want to them that fear him."   Psalm 34:9 (KJV)

"He will bless them that fear the LORD, *both* small and great."
             Psalm 115:13 (KJV)

"By humility *and* the fear of the LORD *are* riches, and honour, and life."   Proverbs 22:4 (KJV)

But if we don't keep our minds on God at all times, we'll miss that gear shifting every time. I knew from the moment Ruth Brown told me to observe my daddy Sam Brown that those gears were shifting. I heard that gear shifting and I made a decision to step on life's accelerator.

Listen, <u>we must keep our minds on God at all times.</u> We'll miss that gear shifting almost every time if we don't. And it's nothing but a habit—listening for that gear shifting—keeping our minds stayed on Him. It will be the best habit you'll ever develop in life. <u>Keeping our minds on God is the habit we want to develop</u>. Keeping our minds off of ungodly things—that is— focus on the positive and leave the negative wherever it was before it entered our minds. Now we are heading in the right direction.

You've got to understand why God wanted me to observe Sam Brown. Sam Brown sent seven of my sisters and brothers to college. This was during the Depression Years. He had four girls in college at the same time, and he was only a farmer. I never heard this farmer say he didn't have any money. Sam Brown paid off his 98-acre farm in the 1920's, when everyone else was losing their farms. And during the Depression, he paid for his children's college tuitions.

I would see him standing in the fields with five vocational agriculture teachers; both African-American and Caucasian

29

brothers came to seek his advice from all over the entire state of North Carolina about farming, or so I thought.

One day I asked him, "How can you spend all that time with county agents and vocational agricultural teachers?" I asked him how could he do it and make money to take care of the farm and the family.

He looked at me real strange, but he had a smile on his face -- a serious smile. I will never forget it.

He said, "I can't afford not to help them."

I said, "You're not making a dime out of this."

> **Be More Concerned about God's People than You are About Yourself**

And then he said to me, "The way you get God's attention in life is to be more concerned about His people than you are about yourself." Then Sam Brown said, "That is why I cannot afford not to help them."

That is why today God is saying to me, "Go feed my chickens." This is why He said that to me. For four years I had fed chickens and turkeys at the Swift Poultry Farm in Greensboro, North Carolina. God knew that on that farm is where I spent much of my *study* time when I was attending North Carolina A & T College. Instead of studying for my classes, I was working at the chicken farm so I could pay my way through college. Guess who spent much of her time with me there? My wife Gladys Lea Brown, the lady who I would not have met if I were not obedient to God's Voice saying to leave my little girlfriend in high school behind.

God is saying to me and to you—what you need in life will come through Me. Bring Me your desires, bring them through Me and I will give you what you need to feed the chickens you got in your house. Maybe you don't have chickens, maybe you have some cats, dogs, or horses. They need food too. God will take care of them and you as well.

I carried that one concept into several fields over my 48-year track record. A man with a C and D transcript from college -- didn't know anything about three different fields, but made millions in each field. If I can do it this way, you can too!

I would see Sam Brown sit with the Bible in his lap early in the morning. Everyone at home was sound asleep, except him and me. He would sit there, the Bible in his lap with tears rolling down his face, but I never did see him turn a page.

"Why are you crying?" I asked him. "And furthermore," I said, "I never see you turn a page."

Here again, he looked at me real strange again. He had a way of doing that. I continued, "The boys talk about reading the Bible, but I never see you reading your Bible. And I never see you turn a page."

He said, "I meditate on the Word. There is a difference."

31

I never forgot what he said. I never forgot it. And then he explained to me how you meditate on the Word.

He said, "You take everything out of the Bible. You make sure every leaf is turned down smooth, i.e., so the Hand of God will move that page to where God wants you to meditate. And then you hold both hands under that Bible, and say, *"In the name of Jesus, Father, let your Word open to where You want me to read. Please Father give me my daily Bread.""*

80   03

.:PAUSE:. Wealth Building Scriptures
Week 1 — My Daily Commitment

1. Sunday - "A new commandment I give unto you, ye
    love one another; as I have loved you, ye also love one
    another." John 12:34 (John 15:12,17); "By this shall all
    men know that ye are my disciples, if ye have love one
    to another." John 13:35.

2. Monday - "And all things, whatsoever ye shall ask in
    prayer, believing, ye shall receive." Matthew 21:22;
    "For verily I say unto you, That whosoever shall say
    unto this mountain, Be thou removed, and be thou cast
    into the sea; and shall not doubt in his heart, but shall
    believe that those things which he saith shall come to
    pass; he shall have whatsoever he saith." Mark 11:23.

3. Tuesday - "Trust in the LORD with all thine heart; and
    lean not unto thine own understanding. In all thy ways
    acknowledge him, and he shall direct thy paths."
    Proverbs 3:5-6.

4. Wednesday - "And it shall come to pass, if thou shalt
    hearken diligently unto the voice of the LORD thy God,
    to observe and to do all his commandments which I
    command thee this day, that the LORD thy God will set
    thee on high above all nations of the earth: and all
    these blessings shall come on thee, and overtake thee,
    for thou shalt hearken unto the voice of the LORD thy
    God." Deuteronomy 28:1-2.

5. Thursday - "And thou shalt love the Lord thy God with all thy heart, and with all thy soul, and with all thy mind, and with all thy strength: this *is* the first commandment." Mark 12:30.

6. Friday - "Trust in the LORD with all thine heart; and lean not unto thine own understanding. In all thy ways acknowledge him, and he shall direct thy paths." Proverbs 3:5-6.

7. Saturday - Blood of Jesus prayer. "And he spake a parable unto them *to this end*, that men ought always to pray, and not to faint;" Luke 18:1; "Watch ye therefore, and pray always, that ye may be accounted worthy to escape all these things that shall come to pass, and to stand before the Son of man." Luke 21:36; "Wherefore also we pray always for you, that our God would count you worthy of *this* calling, and fulfill all the good pleasure of *his* goodness, and the work of faith with power:" 2 Thessalonians 1:11.

8. Bonus - "Greater love hath no man than this, that a man lay down his life for his friends." John 15:13.

9. Bonus - "But his delight *is* in the law of the LORD; and in his law doth he meditate day and night." Psalm 1:2.

(Read Wealth Building Scriptures Aloud—3x Daily)

.:PAUSE:. **W**ealth **B**uilding **T**ips
Week 1 – My Daily Affirmation

1. Sunday - I will join forces and team up with my brothers and sisters of every nation forming partnerships of success.

2. Monday - I make up my mind that every day everything I touch in life from this point forward will turn to gold.

3. Tuesday - I will do extra things to get ahead. I will go beyond what is expected of me.

4. Wednesday - I will make decisions, which change my life for the positive.

5. Thursday - I will apply scripture to my daily living expecting my goals to be accomplished with divine purposes.

6. Friday - When that gear in life shifts, I will know exactly what to do by being prepared to go to the next level.

7. Saturday - I will keep my mind on God at all times. It will be the best habit I will ever develop in life.

8. Bonus - I will get God's attention in life by being more concerned about His people than I am about myself."

9. Bonus - I will meditate on the Word. It will make a difference. I will make a difference.

(Read Wealth Building Tips Aloud-3x Daily)

Chapter 2

Your Personal Success

Using the
P.A.U.S.E. ®
(Practical Application and Use of the Scriptures Everyday)
Wealth Building System

"But as it is written, Eye hath not seen, nor ear heard, neither have entered into the heart of man, the things which God hath prepared for them that love him."

1 Corinthians 2:9

Doing It God's Way®

Chapter 2

Your Personal Success

The Pathway to Your Personal Success

Then **Sam Brown** after showing me how to get the "Daily Bread" looked at me with that strange look on his face and said, "That's the way you get your daily bread." I never forgot that concept.

He said, "I want the daily bread in life."

And I call that concept in my books, cassettes, and CDs, the *Pathway to Success*. Regardless of what you do for a living it works. There is a path in every career field to follow. If you follow these God-purposed paths, they will lead you to your personal success as it does for the leaders in every field. The *Pathway to Your Personal Success* shows you how to follow those paths. It works for every field into which you go regardless of your education level or experience.

Any man or woman, boy or girl, who uses the *Pathway to Your Success* every day, seven days a week, will have success. No man on earth can compete with you unless they are doing it this way. I don't care what you do for a living this works. I don't know about you, but I want everything that's rightfully mine and you should, too.

It's not the color of our skin that holds us back; nor is it our attractiveness or weight. What holds us back are the procedures that we use or do not use; or the choices we make or do not make. These procedures work. They worked very well for me and they will work very well for you also.

When you use this procedure, your Bible will be open to two pages. Read your Bible from left to right, start with the first chapter (or Psalms) which appears on the left. If there is not a chapter (or Psalms) beginning on the left, start with the Psalms or chapter on the right. Complete the chapter (or Psalms) which you started. You may have to turn a page to complete the chapter (or Psalms) — and that's okay.

Read the chapter (or Psalms) three times. Why three times? One time for the Father, one time for the Son, and one time for the Holy Spirit. This gives you the strength and know-how to do God's Will. It takes a lot of strength and know-how to perform and execute the Directives which God gives you. When it falls on the Psalms or the chapters, complete each chapter or each Psalm.

> You Want to Correctly Convey Your Ideas to Your Customers

Read each chapter three times or each Psalm three times. Read them aloud.

Why read them aloud? The answer is two-fold:

1) The purpose of reading them aloud is it gives you a good speaking voice. A good speaking voice is a must to make it in this land. When you speak to your customers they must hear you distinctively so they can not only get the same understanding which you have received over the years, but hear exactly what you are attempting to convey to them with the specific words that you are using. You want to correctly convey your ideas to your customers.

2) You gain power from the words of the author by speaking and believing what God has said in His Word. Let the words become a part of you, a part of your being. Believe what you are reading and put it into action. And become a doer of the God's Word and not just a hearer.

41

<u>Hear the words as you read them and between each reading, lift your hands in praise to God. Thank Him for what He is doing in your life, but do not ask Him for anything. Tell Him how good He has been to you and mean it.</u>

Here are two examples of praise to use at the completion of each reading of each chapter or Psalm. Do this three times; once after each reading of the scripture to which your Bible opens. Here are two examples, which you can use in between each reading. And it doesn't matter which one you use; as long as you use them at the end of each reading. You can use your own as long as they are praise-worthy.

<u>Say:</u>

1) *"Thank you Father for keeping me as the apple of your eye. Thank You Father for hiding me underneath the shadow of Your wings." "If it had not been for you Father, bloody men would have swallowed me up in this earth. Thank You Father."*

When you complete saying this, reach your hands up as far as you can and praise God. Stand up and do this. Don't just sit there, stand up. Standing is praise-worthy, biblical and a little exercise helps us to feel good no matter what we are doing, but especially when we are meditating on the Word.

And let me say this, it doesn't matter which one you use. You can change them around and use the one you would like to use.

Say:

> 2) "Thank You Father for being so good to me. *"You are an awesome God, You are a loving God, You are a kind God, You are a sweet God. My expectation cometh from you. Without You Father, I cannot do anything on this earth."* Thank you for enlarging me when I was in distress."

This is the type of praise which is to be used. We want to: 1) thank Him, then 2) praise Him. My experience has been the more you lift your hands in praise to God, the more blessings will drop from Heaven to you. You cannot fake it until you make it. You have to trust and believe in this. You have to trust and believe God from the top of your head to the tip of your toes. All throughout the Bible, it tells you to trust and believe in God.

King David says, you have to praise Him when times are good, and you have to praise Him when times are bad. Didn't he say this? If you think I praise Him in the church, you should see me praising Him on the job or at home. When we do not see our praises working, do not get into a pity-party too quickly—not at all is my suggestion to you. Try to praise God before your adversity attacks, during an adversity attack, and never get into a pity-party. Pity parties block people's ideas. Praise brings blessings. When you turn your pity-party into a happy state of mind—ideas, direction, and blessings follow. You cannot sell when you are depressed. Remember, jokes can and will take you and your customers out of their bad moments, their bad thoughts, and their pity-parties.

Hightower Road

Hightower Road. Hightower Road Apartments. This is an example of how the *Pathway of Success* worked for me and how it can work for you. I was in my office on Lindhurst Drive, selling 10-15 homes a month. I was the sole salesperson involved in presenting these home sales opportunities to prospective buyers and sellers; no one else was involved in my sales. To this day, I don't know how in the world I did it all but for the LORD. Look at what was going on, and I did it all:

1) Selling 10-15 houses per month, 2) Dealing with the water department telling me I had no water nor sewer rights on the land I had just purchased; the land being the old City Dump, 3) Supervising the manager of our Cascade Cabana Apartments which we owned and managed, 4) Dealing with the Surveyor shooting from Burton Road, 5) And eventually dealing with the property salesman who sold me the property to which water and sewer rights were finally granted, trying to buy the land back from me for double the price.

When you are dealing with this much diversified property management, everyone wants to talk to you. But you don't have time to talk to anyone. You don't have time to think; you are just acting and reacting.

This is how it happened. A man walks into my office. Oh this man could sell; and he was dressed for the occasion. Listen to what this man said to me.

"Mr. Brown, MARTA is coming through in two years. You will make a whole lot of money if you buy this property I have for you."

Boy, did he have my attention. Every Real Estate man wants to make a whole lot of money on a "sweetheart" deal. This sounded like one of those deals to me. It seemed too good to be true. Boy could this man sell. You know we can talk too much and get ourselves in a mess. Sometimes it pays to listen. This man had my attention. I was listening.

He said, "The price is right. $100,000."

You know what they say, "If it looks like it's too good to be true—then it most likely is."

Then he said, "Mr. Brown I got three acres of land on Hightower Road and you can have it for a measly $100,000. The good thing about it is, it is zoned for apartments." He was lying to me, but I did not know it at the time.

He did not have to say anything else. But one thing I want to point to everyone who reads this book, I acted like I didn't know anything about MARTA coming through the area—specifically, right through that property. I knew it already. I knew it because during my *Pathway of Success* time it was revealed to me.

That is doing the Word. I am talking about that Word that God is talking about. Not only was I being shrewd like Jacob with Laban, I was protecting my interests like Abraham with Sarai and the King of Egypt. I was playing a role: the "dumb Negro." He bought it hook, line, and sinker; then I bought the property. I acted as if I did not know MARTA was coming through.

Immediately, after this man left, I carried the good news home to my family. We are supposed to spread the Good News. Well I was spreading the good news about my business transaction to my family. My house filled with the joy of the money I expected to make from MARTA because of this property purchase.

My two sons were around the house singing this song, "Daddy is going to make a whole lot of money. Daddy is going to make a whole lot of money."

I heard my wife tell my oldest son this, "Your daddy is the smartest man who ever walked on this earth."

I even thought so myself until I got to city hall to get the building permit. That is when I discovered that I had bought a piece of land which I had put $100,000 into, money dispersed and the deal closed, only to discover that there was no way to bring in water nor sewer onto the property. The man at city hall who was selling the building permits, said to me.

"Oh that Tim got you didn't he Mr. Brown?"

You can make a mistake with God and He will turn it into a fortune. He was referring to Tim Alexander who sold me the property. <u>You can think you are making a mistake, but don't.</u> Your family may think you are making a mistake, but don't you think that way. <u>Think positively and expect positive results.</u> These sales techniques can turn a fortune. Herman Russell and all the big-time Real Estate men refused to deal with those three acres on Hightower Road. But here is the good news. Don't ever forget it as long as you live on this earth. I did not get into a pity-party. <u>Don't you ever get into a pity-party.</u> Count everything that comes your way as joy.

"My brethren, count it all joy when ye fall into divers temptations; knowing *this*, that the trying of your faith worketh patience. But let patience have *her* perfect work, that ye may be perfect and entire, <u>wanting nothing</u>."

James 1:2-4 (KJV)

I went home, got up early the next morning reaching for my Bible as soon as I got up. That is all I had to do. And it was no more work than drinking a glass of water. I talked to my Heavenly Father just like Christ did when He was sent to this earth. Jesus got up early every morning and talked to His Heavenly Father didn't He?

God asked me, "Have you meditated on My Word this morning?"

I asked Him, "Where do You want me to turn to Father? Show me Father, what to do and how to do it?"

If a man with a C and D transcript can do this kind of stuff that means every man who reads this book can do it too. You will discover that doing the *Pathway to Success*® for your success will be the greatest drink of water that you ever had.

Remember, what may look like a headache is only a blessing in disguise. The Hightower Road apartment home community was finally completed on this property after I got the building plans together, the loan worked out, and the construction overseen, managed, and completed. Two years later in comes MARTA, condemning properties left and right in metro Atlanta—pushing the public transportation issue right through this property, which now has a 60-unit apartment home community sitting on it.

My wife and I netted after everyone got paid off, a net of over $300,000 tax free. Tax free because it was a condemnation project. You do not have to pay taxes on condemned property. And all I had to do was ask Father God who should I get me as an attorney to represent me on this transaction with MARTA. MARTA, the same public transportation company which condemned the land, turned right around and bought this land from me. If I can do it, you can too.

But before I realized that success this is the rest of the story. I knew I needed an attorney to help me fight MARTA over my land which was condemned. I asked Father God what I should do. Guess what my Heavenly Father said to me during the *Pathway to Success*®?

"What about this man from Greensboro North Carolina?" That is all I needed to hear. I contacted J. Kenneth Lee. I told him that I needed his services but I did not have any money to pay him.

"Brown, pay me when you get it," is what J. Kenneth Lee said to me.

He was the attorney from North Carolina who the Lord was talking about. I

Get the

Daily Bread

Out of Life

---

was sending Kenneth Lee documentation of everything that MARTA was doing concerning that property. Everything that MARTA was doing incorrectly Kenneth Lee was receiving in the mail from me and he evaluated everything. And I do mean everything. Leaving appraisal packages in my door, not following the rules and regulation on the appraisal and property condemnation. They were doing sloppy work.

He had researched how they were to condemn properties and conduct appraisals in Georgia and found they were doing much of their work incorrectly—not by the books. Kenneth Lee was one of those people in my life with whom the Lord told me to stick—"Stick with Kenneth Lee."

I had to fly him to Atlanta, Georgia to represent me. J. Kenneth Lee had to file a brief before going to court. He called the judge before coming to Atlanta. Guess what he said to the judge?

"I am not coming down there to talk about appraisals," Kenneth Lee told the judge, "I am coming down there to close MARTA down. When they made the appraisal, condemning the property, they did not do it correctly. They didn't do that and many other things correctly and I know it." Kenneth Lee continued, "And your Honor, tell them if I do not win this in Atlanta, I will win this in Washington, D.C. I am coming down there to shut MARTA down if they do not do the right thing in this case."

Do you know that they would not go to court with this man? MARTA paid me and they paid J. Kenneth Lee an extra $100,000 just to get him out and keep him out of town. He pulled me aside and said, "Brown, I am going to give you $60,000 of the $100,000 and I am going to take $40,000 for my expenses for coming here.

This is a beautiful world in which we are living. You have to know how to use the _Pathway of Success_ to get your personal success. You cannot lose with God and His Son Jesus.

Back to the
Pathway to Success®

When you **do** the Pathway to Success,® hear the words as you read them aloud and in between each reading, lift your hands in praise to your Heavenly Father. Thank Him for what He is doing in your life, good or bad; counting it all joy. Remember, do not ask Him for anything in between each reading. <u>Tell Him how good He has been to you and mean it.</u>

You have to read the scripture three times. Remember this always, the only Ones in the room are God, His Son, and the Holy Spirit and you. You read the scripture three times: one time for the Father, one time for the Son, and one time for the Holy Spirit. This gives you the strength and the know-how to do God's will.

80   03

.:PAUSE:. **W**ealth **B**uilding **S**criptures
Week 2 — My Daily Commitment

1. Sunday - "My voice shalt thou hear in the morning, O LORD; in the morning will I direct my prayer unto thee, and will look up." Psalms 5:3; "Give us this day our daily bread." Matthew 6:11: "Trust in the LORD with all thine heart; and lean not unto thine own understanding. In all thy ways acknowledge him, and he shall direct thy paths." Proverbs 3:5-6.

2. Monday - "My voice shalt thou hear in the morning, O LORD; in the morning will I direct my prayer unto thee, and will look up." Psalms 5:3; "And now I am no more in the world, but these are in the world, and I come to thee. Holy Father, keep through thine own name those whom thou hast given me, that they may be one, as we *are*." John 17:11; "Then said Jesus, Father forgive them; for they know not what they do. And they parted his raiment, and cast lots." Luke 23:34.

3. Tuesday - "*There is* no speech nor language, *where* their voice is not heard." Psalms 19:3; "Then spake Jesus to the multitude, and to his disciples," Matthew 23:1.

4. Wednesday - "And the burden of the LORD shall ye mention no more: for every man's word shall be his burden; for ye have perverted the words of the living God, of the LORD of hosts our God." Jeremiah 23:36; "For by thy words thou shalt be justified, and by thy

words thou shalt be condemned." <u>Matthew 12:37</u>; "For our gospel came not unto you in the word only, but also in power, and in the Holy Ghost, and in much assurance; as ye know what manner of men we were among you for your sake." <u>1 Thessalonians 1:5</u>.

5. Thursday - "Enter into his gates with thanksgiving, and into his courts with praise: be thankful unto him, and bless his name." <u>Psalms 100:4</u>; "Oh that *men* would praise the LORD *for* his goodness, and *for* his wonderful works to the children of men!" <u>Psalm 107:31</u>.

6. Friday - "Praise ye the LORD. Praise ye the name of the LORD; praise *him*, O ye servants of the LORD." <u>Psalms 135:1</u>; "Lift up your hands *in* the sanctuary, and bless the LORD." <u>Psalms 134:2</u>.

7. Saturday - "My brethren, count it all joy when ye fall into divers temptations;" <u>James 1:2</u>.

8. Bonus - Play the role... Joseph story: <u>Genesis 39</u>.

9. Bonus - ..."Princes also did sit *and* speak against me: *but* thy servant did meditate in thy statues." <u>Psalm 119:23</u>; <u>John 8:2</u>; "My hands also will I lift up unto thy commandments, which I have loved; and I will meditate in thy statues." <u>Psalm 119:48</u>.

10. Bonus - "And we know that all things work together for good to them that love God, to them who are the called according to his purpose." <u>Roman 8:28</u>.

(Read Wealth Building Scriptures Aloud-3x Daily)

.:PAUSE:. Wealth Building Tips
Week 2 – My Daily Affirmation

1. Sunday - I will get my daily bread by doing the *Pathway to Success*®.

2. Monday - I will read the Scriptures out loud; not yelling but aloud, in my speaking voice.

3. Tuesday - I will practice speaking properly. I will correctly convey my ideas to my customers.

4. Wednesday - I will gain power from the words of authors when I read their words by reading in my speaking voice and listening to the words.

5. Thursday - The Pathway to Success®. I will hear the words as I read them and between each reading, I will lift my hands in praise to God. I will thank Him for what He is doing in my life, but I will not ask Him for anything. I will tell Him how good He has been to me and I will mean it.

6. Friday - I will lift my hands in praise to God more and expect blessings (opportunity) to drop from Heaven.

7. Saturday - I will not have any "pity parties" which block ideas. I will respond positively to whatever happens.

8. Bonus - I will play the role that needs to be played.

9. Bonus - The Pathway to Success®. I will get up early in the morning reaching for my Bible as soon as I get up.

10. Bonus - I believe good comes from what every person does. I believe there are no mistakes with God.

(Read Wealth Building Tips Aloud-3x Daily)

Chapter 3

Programs for Success

Using the
P.A.U.S.E. ®
(Practical Application and Use of the Scriptures Everyday)
Wealth Building System

"Trust in the LORD with all thine heart; and lean not unto thine own understanding. In all thy ways acknowledge him, and he shall direct thy paths."

Proverbs 3:5-6

Doing It God's Way®

Chapter 3

Programs for Success

Program Number One

Number One Program. I lifted up my eyes and voice to God asking Him to give me <u>my tailor-made church home and tailor-made business program</u>. When you lift your voice and eyes to God asking about that church home that is tailor-made for you and He gives that church to you, then "<u>stick to the plan</u>." God put me in two programs. The <u>number one</u> program God put me in was the "Church Home" that was tailor-made for me and the <u>number two</u> program was J. Douglas Edwards' "Tell It Like It Is" program.

God said to me, "Wherever you go in life, whatever you want to accomplish in life's seminars, when you get back home -- get back on these two programs." The "Church Home" that's tailor-made for you and J. Douglas Edwards's "Tell It Like It Is" program. That J. Douglas Edwards surely could talk some business to you—the "closing your sales" business. Remember, everyone is always selling something.

All churches, all jobs, all businesses, are not tailor-made for me, nor for you. I want to make sure I'm in the church home that's tailor-made for AC Brown. You want to make sure you are in the church home that is tailor-made for you too.

We all should look at it this way – Father God has a plan, a purpose for every individual who walks this earth. We've also got to look at it this way -- if it were not for God, we would not

> Find a
> Church Home
> that is
> Tailor-Made
> for You

be here now alive and walking here on this earth. This kind of language is easy to say, but not easy to believe, and certainly not easy to live for most individuals. You must believe from the top of your head to the bottom of your feet for that mustard seed of faith to activate in your life. I do not deviate from the plan that God gives me, not one inch. And you should not either.

If you try to put your two cents worth in there, and arrange it the way you think it should go, you go nowhere. Or you may go somewhere, but you may not like it when you get there. You will be sitting in the church home <u>that is tailor-made</u> for you or you will be sitting in the church <u>that is not tailor-made</u> for you; not your church home.

In that church home that's tailor-made for you, you can hear one word that will revolutionize your entire life. Or you can be over there in another church home because there is a crowd over there and you miss the word that is tailor-made for you in your true church home to which God told you to go.

<u>Be in the church home that is tailor-made for you.</u> If I can do it this way, you can too and success will be yours!

Program Number Two

Number Two Program. "Tell It Like It Is" The <u>number two</u> program is J. Douglas Edwards' "Tell It Like It Is" program. His program is simply: Tell it like it is. Don't cover up anything. Talk about everything. His program was one of professional motivation through communication. J. Douglas Edwards, at the height of his life experience was considered by many to be the world's greatest sales trainer; working with sales persons at the $100,000 and above sales range, teaching closing techniques and sales approaches.

You must <u>practice your sales approach so that it becomes a part of your personality</u>. You have to relate to people and let them know specifically that you are going to do it this way:

God's Way. To be successful doing it God's way—remember, everyone is selling something all the time. If it is only yourself, you must sell yourself to be successful.

Father God favors prepared individuals. Prepare yourself by knowing and using the Scriptures and by focusing on the positive and not the negative in everything, including yourself. Here are a few:

Pointers to Live by.

    A)   Be real to yourself, your goals, and Father God,

    B)   Study and know your product and your market,

    C)   Focus on the positive things in your life, and practice the repetition of those things,

    D)   Write and re-write your sales pitch to fit your market and your product as perfectly as possible,

    E)   Rehearse your presentation, practicing in front of a mirror, in front of a child, your husband or wife, or in front of one of your peers.

Relate your presentation to the personality of the person who will be in front of you. You have to get serious with your sales approach if you want it to become a part of your personality.

Sales approaches do not work and will not work if you have to turn them off and turn them on. Sales approaches will not work and do not work if you turn them off and on due to your fear, apprehension, unpreparedness, or lack of confidence.

We may want to do it *this* way or we may want to do it *that* way – but we must do it <u>God's Way</u>. What this means is to <u>acknowledge God's contribution in your life</u> (this amounts to praise) during your conversation with the person across from you; the person to whom you are selling. You must practice your sales approach so that it becomes a part of your personality. This doesn't have to be for a life-time but for the season in which you want to have success through high sales volumes.

Study. Know. Rehearse. Engage. Success. <u>Study</u> your market and product. <u>Know</u> your sales approach. <u>Rehearse</u> your presentation. <u>Engage</u> your potential client. <u>Success</u> will be yours.

Do not always stay on the beaten path; try something different. It is often said, insanity is doing things the same way and expecting a different result. Try something new. Consult God first.

Make your goals a part of your personality. Remember, some things you can only do if you own your own business. Some risks you can only take if you own your own business. When you work for others, you must follow their rules which may not relate to selling the way you would do it if you were working for yourself.

Do not allow fear to turn you off and on. Do not let fear turn you off of a proposal, a business deal, a way of life or off of you present path. Stick with your plan—stick to your goals.

Place your goals where you can see them daily—a refrigerator will do just fine. Repeat your plans at least three times a day. Do you have a plan? Stick to that plan and let that plan be God's Plan for you and your business and your family. Do you live life this way?

Here comes the wife. Are you going to stick to God's plan—to God's goals and God's direction given to you and your family during your *Pathway to Success*®? Here comes decision time. Here comes your child; its decision time. Is that God's Plan? Here comes the husband; its decision time. Are you going to stick to your goals—to God's plan? Here comes your boss. Are you going to stick to the plan—to your goals?

God helped me make the decision. God and I have to deal with the consequences of the decision. Since Father God helped me with the decision, God and I are going to make the decision happen; goal by goal, step by step, day by day. Write it down and make it plain and place it on your refrigerator, reviewing it everyday. If I can do it this way, you can too!

We are talking sales approaches here. The head of the household is responsible and must govern himself accordingly by living life God's way – living by God's decisions. Is this your decision or your wife's decision? Is this your decision or your husband's decision? Is this a decision made for a child? Is it your decision or your boss's decision?

Is this your decision or your prospective customer's decision? The man is the head of the household and must know what his family needs. You are the boss of you -- are you operating this way? -- Making your decisions and following them?

Are your decisions, Father God's decisions? Do your decisions have God's will in mind? His goals and objectives?

◦   ◦

.:PAUSE:. Wealth Building Scriptures
Week 3 — My Daily Commitment

1. Sunday - "Trust in the LORD with all thine heart; and lean not unto thine own understanding. In all thy ways acknowledge him, and he shall direct thy paths." Proverbs 3:5-6.

2. Monday - "Know ye not that they which run in a race run all, but one receiveth the prize? So run, that ye may obtain." 1 Corinthians 9:24; "Wherefore seeing we also are compassed about with so great a cloud of witnesses, let us lay aside every weight, and the sin which doth so easily beset *us*, and let us run with patience the race that is set before us," Hebrews 12:1; Ecclesiastes 9:11.

3. Tuesday - Abraham and Sarai (Genesis 12); "And the LORD was with Joseph, and he was a prosperous man; and he was in the house of his master, the Egyptian. And his master saw that the LORD *was* with him, and that the LORD made all that the did to prosper in his hand." Genesis 39:2-3.

4. Wednesday - "Study to shew thyself approved unto God, a workman that needeth not to be ashamed, rightly dividing the word of truth." 2 Timothy 2:15; "My brethren, count it all joy when ye fall into divers temptations;" James 1:2.

5. Thursday - "For even hereunto were ye called: because Christ also suffered for us, leaving us an example, that ye should follow his steps:" 1 Peter 2:21.

6. Friday - "Study to shew thyself approved unto God, a workman that needeth not to be ashamed, rightly dividing the word of truth." 2 Timothy 2:15.

7. Saturday - "After these things the word of the LORD came unto Abram in a vision, saying, Fear not, Abram: I am thy shield, and thy exceeding great reward." Genesis 15:1; "Ye shall not fear them: for the LORD your God he shall fight for you." Deuteronomy 3:22; "And Joshua said unto them, Fear not, nor be dismayed, be strong and of good courage: for thus shall the LORD do to all your enemies against whom ye fight." Joshua 10:25; "Are not five sparrows sold for two farthings, and not one of them is forgotten before God?" Luke 12:6.

8. Bonus - "And the LORD answered me, and said, Write the vision, and make *it* plain upon tables, that he may run that readeth it." Habakkuk 2:2.

(Read Wealth Building Scriptures Aloud-3x Daily)

.:PAUSE:. **W**ealth **B**uilding **T**ips
Week 3 – My Daily Affirmation

1. Sunday - I will attend the "Church Home" that is tailor-made for me. Father God has a plan for my life and applying principles found in this book is a part of that plan.

2. Monday - I will learn and practice the number two program of AC Brown: J. Douglas Edwards' "Tell It Like It Is" program of sales approaches and closes, remembering I am selling something all the time.

3. Tuesday - I will practice my approaches so that they become a part of my personality. I am selling something all the time.

4. Wednesday - I will prepare myself by knowing and using the Scriptures, pointers to live by, and by focusing on the positive and not the negative in everything, including myself.

5. Thursday - I will relate my presentation to the personality of the person who I am selling. I will acknowledge God's contribution in my life by being like Jesus, turning heartbreak and tears into joy.

6. Friday - I will study. I will rehearse. I will engage. I will succeed. I will make my goals a part of my personality.

7. Saturday - I will not allow fear to turn me off and on.

8. Bonus - I will write down my goals and make them plain and place them on my refrigerator, reviewing them daily.

(Read Wealth Building Tips Aloud-3x Daily)

Chapter 4

Look Up

Using the
P.A.U.S.E.®
(Practical Application and Use of the Scriptures Everyday)
Wealth Building System

"While we look not at the things which are seen, but at the things which are not seen: for the things which are seen are temporal; but the things which are not seen are eternal."

2 Corinthians 4:18

Doing It God's Way®

Chapter 4

Look Up

After Army Discharge

Fifteen months to go in the army and my wife was teaching in Fayetteville, NC. We want things, but we often do not act them out. We must walk them out. We talk about faith, but we don't act it out. I acknowledged to God again. Why? I was getting out of the service in 15 months. I said, "Father in the name of Jesus, I will be getting out of service in 15 months. I want to be working in the same location in which my wife is working."

My wife was teaching in Fayetteville, North Carolina.

In three months, she and the principal had some misunderstanding. He fired her right on the spot.

I knew what was happening, but she didn't. She had been there for about five years doing a good job and it happened. God was directing our paths. I knew it, but she didn't know it. She accepted a job immediately in Newbern, North Carolina. Another principal hired her before she could hardly get home.

That summer after I left military service, I went back to A & T College in Greensboro, North Carolina for summer school.

"Brown," my brother-in-law Wilbert Rainer said, "I know you are an agriculture major. Why don't you take some industrial arts courses?"

Immediately, I said, "I believe Wilbert Rainer got something here."

"Take the industrial arts courses," he said. "It won't do anything," Wilbert continued, "but help you in your vocational agriculture courses. All of it is shop work."

I took Wilbert up on it. It wasn't Wilbert Rainer talking—that was God talking. You have to know when God is speaking to you through a person. <u>You can listen and observe and watch and you can see and hear God talking to you and moving in your life.</u>

Every subject I took that summer at A & T College was shop work. Here again that was God directing AC Brown's path. If you acknowledge Me, I will direct your path. Guess what happened at the end of that summer school? Here comes a letter from Newborn, North Carolina. The principal from Newbern, North Carolina was writing me to come down for an interview.

70

He wanted me, a vocational agriculture teacher, to come to be interviewed for an industrial arts teacher job without a cut in salary. I went down. I knew I was going to get the job, because I had acknowledged to God. When I acknowledge God, tell God about a thing, I don't change God's plan. I do exactly what God has

Don't Dilly-Dally When Talking to God about Your Plans

said for me to do. That is all I will do—God's plan. You can't dilly-dally around with God's plans or you plan to fail. Do it God's way.

> "You shall not add unto the word which I command you, neither shall ye diminish *ought* from it, that ye may keep the commandments of the LORD your God which I command you."
>
> Deuteronomy 4:2

I knew Lea and I were going to be in the same town, because I had asked God for it to be that way. But I didn't know we were going to be at the same school. Wasn't that just like God to make it so right?

I worked two years as an Industrial Arts teacher without a cut in salary. If you acknowledge Me, I will direct your path. If you do it any other way, you are always going to think someone owes you something. Yes. You owe yourself something, because you did not acknowledge to God. You went on your own merry way down the road to failure. If you do it any other way other than God's way, you will know that things are just not quite right. Something will be missing. You owe it to yourself to do it God's way—to live life God's way.

Do not think it is the color of your skin? Do not think you are not qualified? I worked in Newbern, North Carolina for two years. My wife worked in Newbern for approximately two and a half years. We decided to move west. Here again, when we put those applications in the mail, I immediately acknowledged God and He directed my path.

My wife immediately got a job in Sedalia, NC near Greensboro, teaching math and chemistry. I *immediately* received a vocational agriculture job in Yadkin County, in Yadkinville, North Carolina; a twelve-month job

Over my 48-year track record, no one has ever had to write a letter of recommendation for me. <u>You have got to understand, God gives the promotions, not man. If you rely on man, you will be in trouble.</u> I'm going to say it for what it's worth, God is a good God, but He is a jealous one.

౬ଓ   ଓଃ

Yadkinville, NC

I **got a vocational agriculture** job in Yadkin County, 80 miles east of Greensboro, North Carolina. I had a year round job with travel pay. I would work at the high school until 12:00 noon and from 12:00 noon until about 5:00 p.m., I was on the farm working. The principal of the Yadkin County High School and the Superintendent of Schools had a good time laughing at my "C" and "D" transcript when I went to apply for the job. They sat there and laughed right in front of me. Can you believe that?

They only hired me for one year. They did not believe I had the qualifications to teach vocational agriculture in the Yadkin County High School. Understand me now, they only hired me for one year. Immediately when I walked out of the office, I knew that they wanted to try me out to see if I had the qualifications to teach vocational agricultural or fail at it.

> Stop Sitting on the Sidelines
>
> Life will Take on a New Meaning

There are a lot of people sitting on the sidelines. If they knew how to acknowledge God in everything they do in life, life would take on a new meaning. When you follow the Wealth Building Tips and Scriptures at the end of each chapter you will learn a plethora of knowledge. I'm so thankful that Sam

73

Brown started me out on the right track before he died.

When I walked out of that principal's office with the Superintendent of Schools standing there, I acknowledged God to be the best vocational agricultural instructor that ever walked into a school in North Carolina. Now I want you to understand that this was a new vocational agricultural department. This was the first year for a new teacher, AC Brown and his new farm boys.

The Contest

There was a contest planned for the end of the school year. Vocational agricultural teachers and their farm boys came to the Yadkin County High School from all over the entire state of North Carolina; twenty-five high schools participated.

That's right. The 25th one was Yadkin County High School. There were five areas in which the farm boys participated. One of the areas was quartet singing. I didn't know anything about singing. My job as a vocational agricultural teacher was to work at the high school until one o'clock and head to the farm to work with the farmers. But in the meantime, I had a serious problem. I had to put that quartet together.

So I told a local music teacher about my problem. She told me to bring the boys by in the afternoon on Fridays to practice.

"I won't charge you a thing," she said. "I will be glad to do it."

All we have to do is be a willing vessel and God will take care of everything else; just go out there and do it.

It took very little effort on my part to make our program blossom.

Not only did the music teacher get them to vocalize in tune, but she also told them what to wear. Those black shiny patent leather shoes, black pants and coats went well with my choreography. They broke out there singing, "Oh, Donna." The big afros blowing in the wind, those four farm boys glided onto the stage, wailing away on *"Oh, Donna."* The crowd went wild.

Ladies and gentlemen you may be surprised at what you can get done when you put God first in your life. Ask and it shall be given you, seek and you shall find.

Guess who was there at the contest? The Principal of the Yadkin County High School and Superintendent of Schools. The same ones who had had such a good time laughing at my transcript. Remember they only hired me for one year. Guess what took place that day?

The Yadkin County High School farm boys took all five areas in the state of North Carolina. Vocational agricultural teachers that had been teaching for years, some of them 20 and 30 years watched the Yadkin County High School farm boys walk away with the awards. Those boys had only been taking the subject for nine months. If you acknowledge Me, I will direct your path. But you can't dilly-dally around. When

75

you do it the way I teach it, you got to mean business. Take acknowledging God as serious business. I know that it is serious business and you should treat it as serious business also.

Believe in yourself when others do not believe in you. If you believe in yourself, others have a tendency to believe in you also. Grades do not mean anything when you have Father God behind you. If I can do it this way, you can too! Believe.

Serious Business

Every job I go on, every business I open, and every church I join, I treat as serious business. Doing the *Pathway to Success*® every morning around three o'clock, I also treat as serious business. This is the way, along with the way my daddy Sam Brown operated, is the way and the best way we are going to go to the "Promised Land". Reading his Bible and working with those farmers and those vocational agricultural teachers and county agents helped my daddy live in the "Promised Land" during tough economic times.

If my daddy Sam Brown went to the "Promised Land" while he was living, you can too. How did he do it? Be more concerned about God's people than you are about yourself. I know you may not be a farmer, I'm not a farmer either but when you read my books and play my cassettes and CD's, you

76

are going to discover I went into several fields and succeeded in every field. If I can do it this way you can too.

That Principal at the Yadkin County High School got so angry with me, he didn't speak to me for the remainder of that school year. He didn't speak to me until the following school year. He never did stand up in front of the student body to congratulate the farm boys although this was their first year in the vocational agricultural department.

Three days before school opened, the Principal came to me and said, "Mr. Brown we're going to change things around this year." He continued, "We are not going out on the farm much this year. I want you to stick around the school and help me load the school buses."

I was walking away from him but made an about-face. I made an about-face and went back to him. After I walked about three feet from him, I looked him dead in the eyes.

I said, "BT, here are your keys. I'm not loading any school buses. The state sent me here to teach vocational agricultural and I'm leaving." I continued, "I want you to know, don't get the idea I'm ever going to ask you to write me a letter of recommendation, because I will not need it. <u>I work for God and God works for me. God gives the promotions not man.</u>"

I walked out of that school and I was just thinking the other day I don't even believe I went back and got my last check.

Every job I go on, every business I open, every church I join when I acknowledge to God, I take it as serious business. I don't dilly-dally. A prizefighter does not go into the ring thinking he is going to lose. <u>When you attempt a thing, know that God wants you to succeed in it.</u> <u>He wants us to expect to win.</u> So go into that ring with a winning attitude. I'm going at it for everything it is worth. That is the way and the only way you are going to succeed in your endeavors. <u>God gives the promotions and that is why I do not ever move away from Him.</u> I don't know how He does it, but He keeps His eye on everyone.

You are not getting by with anything. He sees everything you do. He knows how you think. He even knows what you are thinking right now. He knows what you are thinking about concerning this course right now also. You can't fool him. "If you acknowledge Me in all your ways, I will direct your paths." Proverbs 3:5-6

Forgiveness
(Proverb 20:22)

Forgiveness is a key to success in any field. Know that there are things in our lives, which we have done, for which we should seek forgiveness. It is important that we first and foremost forgive ourselves and ask the Lord for forgiveness. Remember to request forgiveness for the offended party or parties.

Once you clear your consciousness of any negative thoughts, flashes, emotions, any guilt, shame, or unforgiveness, you can have a clearer focus towards your personal goals. Your clear conscious will allow you to smile as you carry your positive mental attitude into your day from its very beginning. Your positive attitude will allow you to see your potential as victory and to see your challenges as opportunities for victory through learning experiences.

Do any of you have anything out there you think you didn't do which you don't have to ask forgiveness for? Has anyone been perfect on this earth? Has anyone done no wrong at some point in their lives? Are there things in your life for which you need to ask forgiveness? Is there anything wrong which you have done? Do I have the mind of a Pharisee?

We think we have to have done something wrong to have to ask for forgiveness. That is what we think. <u>If we do not ask for forgiveness for all things, we are not going to accomplish our "bigger-than-expected" goals</u>.

"Thine eye shall not pity him, but thou shalt put away *the guilt of* innocent blood from Israel, that it may go well with thee."

Deuteronomy 19:13

<u>Until we do it, until we ask for forgiveness for all things, we are not going to accomplish great things</u>. Consider asking for forgiveness for things for which you think you have not done. I would go ask for forgiveness for a thing, whether I thought I had done something wrong to someone or not.

Personally, I attempt to keep a "clean slate" on my conscious. That "clean slate," <u>my clean conscious allows me to</u>

have the confidence to pursue and attain my sales and personal short-term and long-term goals. That is the way and the only way we are going to go to the "Promised Land"— keeping a "clean conscious" by forgiving others and asking for forgiveness even if we are not wrong. We are going to have to straighten it out now or straighten it out when we die. We will have to straighten it out in the next world, if we do not straighten it out here. But believe you me, it will get straight either on this earth or in heaven; or somewhere else.

I have had several people come to me asking for forgiveness for things, which happened years ago. I look up at night and I see them asking for forgiveness. If you got anything out there that you are not sure about, make sure you go to those people and ask for forgiveness. You may be thinking that you didn't do it. They did it. But are you angry about it? That is just as bad. Go phone them and ask for forgiveness; or write them a letter and have the courage to mail it. Remember, forgiveness is the main goal of this exercise—your forgiveness—your forgiving yourself will free your conscious.

My family had not invited me to a family reunion for twelve years. This is what happened to cause them to feel and act this way. I will tell you exactly what took place.

I was at a double funeral for a brother and a sister. I must admit it really was a sad occasion. During the funeral, I wanted everyone who seemed sad to find joy in this homecoming occasion. I teased different funeral home members and family members with humor for relief. I wasn't scheduled to give an eulogy, but I was asked to say something; so I did. I had to get up there at that funeral, that second death, and talk about what was on my mind.

Just before speaking I was sitting there between my sister, Grady and another family member, Ida Mae, who was the funeral director. They were just wailing tears. Ida Mae passed Grady a facial tissue.

I said loud enough for my neighbors to hear, "Ida Mae why are you passing my sister a tissue? You just collected money on two dead bodies from the same family in one week. Knock it off the bill."

My sister Grady immediately slapped on the brakes and stopped crying.

Then I said to the people, "Didn't Jesus go out there and practice turning tears into joy."

The Holy Spirit had been speaking to me while I was sitting there listening and watching everything. I was receiving an epiphany. I was to give up my Real Estate career and work on God's program which I am bringing to you through this book. The Wealth Building System—P.A.U.S.E.: Practical Application and Use of the Scriptures Everyday. I have worked on this program in various stages of development for over twenty years.

The Lord told me that if I did not do His program that I would be like my brother and sister lying there in those coffins. That black hearse will pull up to the curb and my coffin, covered with flowers would be put inside while the choir sang, *"Nearer my God to thee."*

Boy, during my eulogy, my family members did not like what I had to say. I told them how God was watching this scene here at the funeral. How many had purchased new clothes for the occasion while not considering visiting my sister or brother while they were ill and laid up. How family members had leased cars for the occasion or purchased new cars for the occasion. I railed on them about showing false compassion when <u>compassion is walked out day in and day out with love expressed in actions, large and small.</u>

Enroute to the cemetery, the limousine was packed with sisters and sister-in-laws. About eighty-five cars were in the lineup. People were there from the north, the south, the east and the west. Only two men were in the limousine. I was sitting crouched over since it was so crowded. Everyone was quiet, solemn, sad and withdrawn. This was an "AC" moment; a time to walk the walk of Jesus.

I said, "Why don't you open this limousine up to eighty-five miles per hour and air this thing out."

"If I do everybody is going to be afraid that they are going to die," said the driver.

From that moment on, conversation, talking, and joking happened until we reached the cemetery. You are supposed to have fun at a funeral; rejoice in the memories of the deceased. Celebrate their lives and usher them into Heaven.

They left that church that day and didn't invite me to family reunions for twelve years. I got angry about it, but you know I had to go and ask for forgiveness before I could bring this course to the nation and the world.

Many simply sit there and say, "Well they did it -- I didn't." Regardless of who started it. Regardless of who is supposed to finish it. Regardless of which way your emotions go concerning it. I wouldn't take the chance. I wouldn't let any man on this earth stop my progress. <u>I would not allow any man on this earth stop my progress by my not asking forgiveness for an offense from me.</u> I wouldn't do it. I would not take the chance. When you start practicing the PAUSE Wealth Building System's Wealth Building Scriptures and Tips which I learned over the course of my 48 year track record of accomplishment, you will make more money than you know what to do with.

ℬ   ℭ

.:PAUSE:. **W**ealth **B**uilding **S**criptures
Week **4** — My Daily Commitment

1. Sunday - "Let not your heart be troubled: ye believe in God, believe also I me." John 14:1; "At that day ye shall know that I *am* in my Father, and ye in me, and I in you." John 14:20; "For it is not ye that speak, but the Spirit of your Father which speaketh in you." Matthew 10:20; "Christ in you is hope for glory." Colossians 1:27.

2. Monday - "For even hereunto were ye called: because Christ also suffered for us, leaving us an example, that ye should follow his steps:" 1 Peter 2:21.

3. Tuesday - "The heavens declare the glory of God; and the firmament sheweth his handywork." Psalm 19:1; "Thou shalt also be a crown of glory in the hand of the LORD, and a royal diadem in the hand of thy God." Isaiah 62:3; "The voice of the LORD *is* upon the waters: the God of glory thundereth: the LORD *is* upon many waters." Psalm 29:3.

4. Wednesday - "The earth *is* the LORD'S, and the fullness thereof; the world, and they that dwell therein." Psalm 24:1; "But seek ye first the kingdom of God, and his righteousness; and all these things shall be added unto you." Matthew 6:33; "Commit thy way unto the LORD; trust also in him; and he shall bring *it* to pass." Psalm 37:5.

5. Thursday - "Greater love hath no man than this, that a

man lay down his life for his friends." John 15:13; "A
new commandment I give unto you, ye love one
another; as I have loved you, ye also love one another."
John 12:34; John 15:12,17; "By this shall all *men* know
that ye are my disciples, if ye have love one to another."
John 13:35.

6. Friday - "One God and Father of all, who *is* above all,
and through all, and in you all." Ephesians 4:6; "For
whatsoever is born of God overcometh the world: and
this is the victory that overcometh the world, *even* our
faith." 1 John 5:4.

7. Saturday - "Say not thou, I will recompense evil; but
wait on the LORD, and he shall save thee." Proverb
20:22; "Then said Jesus, 'Father forgive them; for they
know not what they do.' And they parted his raiment,
and cast lots." Luke 23:34; "For if ye forgive men their
trespasses, your heavenly Father will also forgive you:
but if ye forgive not men their trespasses, neither will
your Father forgive your trespasses." Matthew 6:14-15.

8. Bonus - "A new commandment I give unto you, ye love
one another; as I have loved you, ye also love one
another." John 12:34 (John 15:12,17).

(Read Wealth Building Scriptures Aloud-3x Daily)

.:PAUSE:. Wealth Building Tips
Week 4 – My Daily Affirmation

1. Sunday – Jesus believes in me. I will believe in myself when others do not believe in me. Others believe in me when I believe in myself.

2. Monday – I realize my actions are moving me towards the things I want. I will direct my actions towards my goals with purpose. I will walk towards my goals.

3. Tuesday – I will hear, observe, touch, watch, smell, see, feel, and experience Father God talking and moving in my life.

4. Wednesday – I will understand that God gives the promotions, not man. I will rely on Father God.

5. Thursday – I will be more concerned about God's people than I am about myself.

6. Friday – I will attempt my aspirations knowing that Father God wants me to succeed in them. I know He wants me to expect to win, therefore I do.

7. Saturday – I will keep a "clean conscious" by forgiving and asking forgiveness. I will ask for forgiveness for all things, and I will accomplish my "bigger-than-expected" goals. I will forgive others and myself so my conscious will be free.

8. Bonus - I will walk with compassion day in and day out, expressed through love in actions large and small.

(Read Wealth Building Tips Aloud-3x Daily)

Chapter 5

Vision

Using the
P.A.U.S.E. ®
(Practical Application and Use of the Scriptures Everyday)
Wealth Building System

"And I say unto you, That if two of you shall agree on earth as touching any thing that they shall ask, it shall be done for them of my Father which is in heaven."

Matthew 18:19

Doing It God's Way®

Chapter 5

Vision

A Home Builder

I **wanted** to be a home builder. All I had to do was <u>open</u> <u>my mouth and look to Heaven and ask Father God to</u> <u>teach me how to be a homebuilder</u>. The answer I received:

"Study how to be a homebuilder under your brother-in-law, Bruce Ruffin."

At the time, there were many builders in Greensboro, North Carolina who were better or worst than Bruce Ruffin. Bruce was the man for the job. I arranged my schedule to stick with Bruce. Bruce was one of those people who God told me to stick with. And I did. Like I said, if you change God's program, everything you touch will backfire. You can't change it. Don't even try.

Just take it one step at a time. And when success comes, it's going to come so fast -- just like snowflakes falling from the sky. I even surpassed Bruce Ruffin as a builder, but we never lost our friendship.

Do not Deviate from God's Plan for Your Life

If God sends you to someone and you don't like what they're doing and you get angry, you're not going to be happy with the circumstances which may follow. When I got ready to go into the big-time building business, all I had to do was open my mouth and ask God aloud.

"Send me someone to do all my financing." That's me talking to God.

In walks RJ Hancock after two years of waiting. This was not one of those "immediate" deals; this was a "wait" deal. Remember, "Wait on the Lord." RJ Hancock came in as though it was supposed to happen the way it did, but I had waited for two years. It happened right on schedule too.

You've got to be patient. You've got to do this thing (your project, your business, your goals, your aspirations) the way God wants it done -- not the way "me, myself, and I" wants it done. If I do it my way, God has done nothing. If I do it God's way, God has done everything, but my part. He tells us so clearly. *"I'll be on your right side. I'll go in front of you."*

"A thousand shall fall at thy side, and ten thousand at thy right hand; *but* it shall not come nigh thee."

Psalm 91:7

Oh, He means it! Two years passed as I waited. You have got to want it so badly that you allow nothing to change your path; allow nothing to change the way Father God has told you to proceed.

During those two years, I attended a church home that was tailor-made for AC Brown. I sat there and listened to those sermons that were tailor-made for me. Suppose I had gone to another church that "old Charles" told me about instead of my tailor-made Church Home?

Do you think I could spread out a track record like this doing it my way? No, not if I disobeyed God. If I've got to do it this way, you've got to do it this way too. Remember, doing it this way, landed me a million dollars three times. It didn't land in my lap, I had to <u>go out there and work for it</u>. And you do too!

Cigarette Factory

T<u>he way</u> you go to the "Promised Land" is to follow <u>Christ.</u> I was working at a cigarette factory from 11:00 pm to 7:00 am in the morning inhaling tobacco dust in Greensboro, North Carolina. While I inhaled tobacco dust, I imagined building houses; single-family homes at first, then

91

sub-divisions, apartments and more. I could see homes being built by AC Brown. I imagined homes being built by AC Brown. I could see subdivisions being developed by AC Brown. I imagined subdivisions being developed by AC Brown.

God had told me to "stick with Bruce." And God told me "to ride with him in his truck and talk building houses all day long."

This is the interesting part, God told me to go home after the cigarette factory job, get two hours of rest then ride with Bruce. Mind you He didn't say sleep, but "rest". Rest: not look at television, not even pick up the newspaper; "quiet time". I was obedient to what God told me to do. I rode with Bruce for days, and weeks, then months. We talked building houses and God and His Son Jesus all day long. I learned a lot. I believe Bruce did too.

The newly formed Brown Construction Company was across the street from A &T College. It meant a lot to me to have an office across the street from where I graduated from college. Bruce's office was across town. One day just out of the blue, in walks RJ Hancock. RJ had been talking with Bruce about building and financing. He also talked to Bruce concerning money. RJ came by to check me out. He wanted to make sure that I was a man that he could trust to pay him back if he loaned me money.

The Bible says without vision man will perish. RJ Hancock needed what Bruce Ruffin and I had: our "know-how," our building "know-how." Bruce Ruffin and I needed what RJ Hancock had: m-o-n-e-y. I got financing on just a handshake; no credit report nor Dun and Bradstreet rating. We didn't have to put anything up as collateral. <u>RJ had what we wanted and we had what RJ wanted.</u> That is why it was so easy.

<u>If you have the "know-how" life can be easier. There are many people in your life who have what you need. There are also other people in your life who need what you have. Study to prepare for life.</u> Study to prepare to sell your Heavenly Father and yourself. *"Study to show yourself approved."*

This is the way God does it. Doesn't He say, *"I will bring you into a wealthy place?"*

Oh, He means it. When RJ Hancock started loaning us millions of dollars, he immediately set up an appointment to meet with Bruce Ruffin and I every Friday afternoon at 3:00 o'clock. He would ask us many questions. He was in the lumber business, but he never asked questions relating to the lumber business -- <u>never</u>! Not one question ever about the lumber business. Bruce and I were too close to the forest to see the trees, but RJ would soon show them to us as lumber.

It's right in the Bible. *"Ask and it shall be given you. Seek and ye shall find. Knock and it shall be opened unto you. For every one that asketh, receiveth. He that seeketh, findeth. And to him that knocketh, it shall be opened."* RJ was asking a ton of questions about building—not about lumber mind you— but about building houses.

"Bruce," he would ask, "what do you think about *this* concerning the building business?"

"Brown," he would ask me, "what do you think about *that* concerning the building business?"

Several months slipped by—nine months in fact. Every Friday, right on time, RJ showed up with a check and with an ear for listening. He listened to us talking about building houses. Bruce and I talked our heads off. We loved to see RJ coming even though we knew we were paying a high interest rate on Mr. Hancock's money. Bruce Ruffin knew he was paying a high interest rate too. <u>But we had to get started somehow.</u> <u>And you've got to get started also.</u>

What we didn't know was the high interest rate was a smoke screen for what RJ was really doing; what he was doing to us and what we were doing to ourselves.

Use good insight and proper planning to secure your future.

One day I was at the bank closing one of RJ Hancock's transactions. RJ Hancock never did go to the bank. Big time operators do not have to go to the bank. They pick up their telephones and tell the banker what to do.

We closed different transactions for approximately nine months. Life was good. Life was great! One Friday afternoon at 3:00 o'clock, RJ Hancock came in very excited. When this was going on—when RJ Hancock was coming by every Friday afternoon—he would ask many questions like this.

"Brown, Bruce, where do you find these good building contractors? How do you pay them so they will work?"

Bruce Ruffin and I would sit there talking our heads off— singing our heads off like to freed canaries. Remember this, <u>money will loosen lips</u>. We loved to see RJ Hancock come. He brought the money, which loosened our lips, and we loved him for it.

Work on God's Plan for Your Life

Like I said, this one Friday RJ Hancock invited us to go with him to Chapel Hill. He was dressed to the "T." He was all excited as we entered this subdivision in Chapel Hill, North Carolina. We saw hundreds of houses under construction – signs swinging everywhere – "RJ Hancock Construction Company."

My brother-in-law got really angry with RJ Hancock. He was in the back seat of the car steaming mad. Bruce couldn't see it like I could see it. This is what Bruce said to me.

"Mr. Hancock has stolen all of our ideas."

<u>Like I said, if God sends someone to see you like RJ Hancock and you get angry because of something you do not like, you're not going to be happy with the outcome.</u> God had sent RJ Hancock to get me started in my goal; my dream of building houses. RJ had done just that: gotten me started. I went on to win the prestigious North Carolina Home Builders

Association "Parade of Homes" Home of the Year located today in Greensboro, North Carolina.

Don't make God's people angry. If you do you're not going to be happy with the outcome. I got what I wanted – a start in the building business. And Bruce Ruffin had more money to spend than he knew what to do with.

Learn to Encourage Yourself

Several months slipped by after Bruce Ruffin said to Mr. Hancock, "You have stolen all our ideas."

Bruce was not laughing and God saw that. Several more months slipped by -- Bruce was murdered.

Forgiveness in any and all of life's situations is extremely important. Learn to forgive. If you cannot forget, at least learn to forgive. Bruce Ruffin was considered by many to be "the professional" to teach you how to build. Oh, Bruce Ruffin could build some homes and he did.

৪০   ৫৪

This particular morning in comes a new situation. This morning the banker called me up. This is what he said.

"Mr. Brown, if you can show me $10,000 in your checking account, you will not need RJ Hancock's services anymore."

That wasn't the banker—it was God using him. That was not the banker talking that morning, it was God. The gear shifted that morning. I made one more trip to RJ Hancock's office and borrowed the $10,000. I bid him farewell on that day.

I am saying something which I know: If you want to make it in this land, you have to do something. If you do nothing, you will accomplish the same: N-O-T-H-I-N-G, nothing. Before we can accomplish anything for God, we have to have the guts and the nerve to move in His direction for you. You have to "prime the pump" with something to get something. You have to "prime the pump" for someone to help. That someone may be you, your job, your career, your life.

From that day to this day, I haven't had to use the services of RJ Hancock anymore. If I can do it this way, you can too!

A New Situation

Let me introduce you to my contractor Johnny Langston. If you do not understand anything I have said, please understand this one thing. This Caucasian brother Johnny Langston built thousands of homes for me. He developed subdivisions. We built the Brown Construction Company office building directly across the street, in front of A & T College which is a university now.

I used to drive up to the Brown Construction Company every morning and I would look over at A & T College and wave at my "C" and "D" transcript -- making tons of money! If I can do it this way, you can too!

I had to encourage myself. When no one out there encourages you, know this: <u>you must depend on God and yourself for encouragement. You've got to encourage yourself, when no one else will.</u>

Like I said, Johnny, this Caucasian brother built thousands of homes for me. He was running four crews. But Johnny Langston and I had to come together in love and truth, seven days a week. That's the way you get "big-time," by coming together. This is what took place.

We Have to Follow God's Instruction to the Letter

I was at my peak as a builder. One of my competitors filed a complaint against me. And this was the complaint: "You are building out of your price range." My license only covered me to build homes up to $80,000 in value. This doctor persuaded me to build this home that cost $300,000. I had got the home halfway finished. Here comes the state department from Raleigh, North Carolina putting a big condemned sign on the home: "Cease All Construction."

AC Brown who didn't do anything in math at A & T College now has a challenge. Now he's got to go to Raleigh, North Carolina and take a math test of 125 math problems – nothing but estimating lumber materials.

God kept talking. He said, "Carry Johnny with you. One of you can pass this test."

God kept on talking that morning.

"You and Johnny," He said, "the Caucasian brother are to study at night when you get off work. Study in love and in truth, seven days a week. You've got two weeks to get ready. Do it."

Remember this always. <u>You have got to follow God's instructions to the letter.</u> For 48 years I have done it this way. If you don't do it this way, you'll never get the real promises of God. <u>Never leave anything out</u> or you will never get the real promises of God and you will live a short life. <u>You've got to obey God</u>. What you leave out may be important to God. This is His world and we are only passing through it.

I learned more about Johnny Langston in those two weeks than I had known for a period of twelve years. We studied at his home. Johnny would put on a pot of coffee and we would sit there until 1 or 2 am in the morning. We hugged one another and we prayed together.

Oh, I knew we had the exam in the bag because Johnny Langston could figure building materials so close he could put the leftovers in the trunk of his automobile. But I didn't know about AC Brown. That Monday morning we headed to Raleigh, North Carolina. When Johnny started taking his examination, he received a telephone call from home. His wife had passed. You know God knew this was going to happen.

Well, I had to do it—I had to pass this test. All I had to do was open my mouth to God and ask Him right there in the classroom. I looked up at the ceiling and said to God.

Work Together in Unity Pray for One Another

"I did it exactly the way you said do it."

I didn't hear from God. I sat there waiting. God didn't say a word. I waited some more. I sat there and waited, then the answers started coming to me like snowflakes from the sky. The answers, the procedures, how to work those math problems, came as fast as I could write. This was all I needed to pass this exam. If you do it the way God lays it out, you won't have to have an answer. It's coming.

> "You shall not add unto the word which I command you, neither shall ye diminish *ought* from it, that ye may keep the commandments of the LORD your God which I command you."
>
> Deuteronomy 4:2

Suppose I had not teamed up with Johnny in love and truth seven days a week? Suppose I did not follow God's instructions? Suppose I was one of those people who do not believe people hear from God? We want things to take place, but often we do not follow what God wants us to do.

When I finished taking that examination, the instructor said, "Mr. Brown, since you're here, let me grade your paper."

Why not? I did it exactly the way God -- who owns it all -- said to do it.

The instructor finished grading my paper and he said, "Mr. Brown, why haven't you been here before?"

"I didn't need to come before," I replied, "I came when I had to come." That is the way I have been doing it.

He said, "You can figure building materials so close, you can put the leftovers in the trunk of an automobile."

Understand
These Principles

I **want you to think here** for a moment. I want you to do some serious thinking here. Just think about this one thing. In about every home across this land, there are one, two, or there could be three slow learners. They can't get it together. When they understand these principles I teach you, their lives are going to take on a new meaning when they follow the Wealth Building Tips and Scriptures at the end of each chapter and follow the procedures I have followed and which I teach you. One scripture and tip for every day of the week for sixteen weeks. You'll make more money with these concepts I'm teaching than you'll know what to do with; you and everyone in your household.

But you can't deviate from the plan. You're going to have to do it the way I teach you. In my books and cassettes and CDs, I teach you how to use these principles of success, Doing It God's Way®.

When I was building houses in Greensboro, North Carolina, I got tired of building houses. I opened my mouth and I asked God to teach me how to be a real estate salesperson. I left Greensboro, North Carolina. I arrived in Atlanta, Georgia; I thought I was there to build houses. I even organized the Medallion Construction Company. I could not get anyone to talk to me about the Medallion Construction Company or building houses.

Oh, you've got to mean business when you open your mouth to God. If you don't mean business and don't get ready for the assignment, you're going to be delayed in achieving your goals. I walked around Atlanta, Georgia for months like I was a dead man. One night I asked God what was wrong.

He said, "I thought you said you wanted to be a real estate salesperson."

I didn't have to ask anything else of God that night. I knew the deal. He brought to my remembrance that which I had asked Him before arriving in Atlanta.

I got my real estate license real quickly. My first commission was $100. That doesn't sound like that's God's program, does it? That soon changed and money started coming in, but Frank Ward and his wife, Patsy were not making much money.

I had to go back to the drawing board and ask God again. "Why? Why wasn't my Caucasian brother, Frank Ward making much money." They were doing all of my finances.

I was more concerned for Frank and Patsy, than for myself. That is the way to get God's attention. My experience has shown me over the years that this is true. You see how I asked God. I asked Him being genuinely more concerned for the Ward family – I believe this got God's attention.

I got an answer immediately, because I said, "The Caucasian brother and I are not making much money." The answer came back immediately due to my genuine concern for my fellow human being. It goes back to Sam Brown saying, "The way to get God's attention is to be more concerned about others than for yourself." In the words of Jesus, "Love one another as I have loved you."

God said, "One of you have got to be willing and not afraid to come together in love and truth seven days a week. If you don't do it, you're not going to make any money."

God was not just talking to AC Brown, He was talking to all of us. There are two situations here -- Johnny Langston, the contractor was Caucasian and Frank Ward, the mortgage officer was also Caucasian--coming together with AC Brown, the African American. What God was saying is that we all have to come together in unity so we can all make money together.

Look what happened when the sports world came together. They have not been together all the time. You know the sports world used to look differently than it does today.

Jackie Robinson was peeping through the fence saying. "Let me play professional baseball."

Look what happened when Jackie got out there and started stealing those bases. Look out there today.

God is sending me with a message to every man, every woman, every boy, and every girl. We've got to come together whether we want to do it or not. You know how God told me how He is going to solve this race problem? The ministers of churches and the owners of businesses are going to have to come together in love and truth whether they want to or not.

We are going to have to come together in love and truth seven days a week. I mean it. <u>When I hear that voice, I don't sit there and wonder who it is, I go into action.</u> If you do not do it that way, you will wonder who received the real promises of God because you will know that you did not.

ॐ   ☙

God Owns Everything

God owns everything. Every day we're going through a training program which is preparing us for the next level. I immediately invited Frank and Patsy Ward to dinner that night. The appointment was for seven o'clock and they had not arrived. My wife and I sat there. We waited thirty minutes. We ordered our meal.

We had just about finished eating when I saw them coming in, walking real fast. I stood up. When you take action and take that first step, God's going to put the words in your mouth. I didn't know what I was going to say when I stood up, but I stood up.

"Frank," I said, "you and Patsy have hung out with us so much you have stolen our bad habit of being late."

From that day, for a period of twenty some years, money dropped like snowflakes falling from the sky.

We started going out together on weekends. We even joined the Skylark Club in Atlanta, and we flew all over America on the weekends. We didn't just party or "blue goose" on these trips -- no! We studied financing together in love and truth on the weekends during those trips; and we would be ready to go back to work when we got back to the office. You will be surprised at what happens when you come together in love and truth with the people with whom you work. You will be surprised at what happens – what God will do when you work together in love and truth with your fellow human beings.

If Frank Ward got a rejection on one of my real estate cases, I was Frank's backup. We would sit down just like two medical doctors discussing a patient's case together. We never lost a single real estate transaction. If I can do it this way, you can too! Come together!

Come Together in Love and Truth

What's the big deal? You've tried everything else, why not come together? Is there a forgiveness issue here that needs to be addressed? The promises of God will start dropping just like snowflakes falling from the sky. But always remember what God said to AC Brown.

"What one of you is going to have to do is, not be afraid. If you're not afraid, I'll show you something."

So don't you be afraid to do what I am imparting into you concerning building your wealth; both your spiritual wealth and your personal wealth. Oh, you will make more money with this program that I am bringing you than you will know what to do with. Try it – it works.

80 ଔ

Listen, when I first came to Atlanta, Georgia my first commission was only $100. Because of his concern, my real estate broker, Lonnie Fuller on Hunter Street, called my wife and I into his office.

Lonnie said, "Mr. Brown, you need to let your wife sell Real Estate." "You've got two sons you've got to take care of." He continued, "Y'all going to starve."

This was during the time of "white flight" in Atlanta neighborhoods. He said that we should co-op with Stovall; meaning Stovall and I would be splitting the commission.

"Please," he went on, "do not go to Cascade Heights and try to list properties. They'll lynch you over there. We just had a barricade here."

God was talking to me at the same time the broker was talking. I excused myself to go to the water fountain. I did not need a drink of water but was really getting to a more quiet location so I could hear what God was saying.

God said, "Brown, when you move in the Cascade area, don't put up a sign until you get the whole street."

Oh, I do it exactly the way God says to do it. I do not deviate. If you do not go along with what God tells you to do, life may not turn out the way you expect it to be. This is your day. Live life "Doing it God's Way." Get involved, join life. Make a God decision. Stop being a passive observer in life and be an active participant. Do it the way I teach you and success will be yours.

When I went up with that whole street of signs I did not hear the name Stovall mentioned again; Lonnie sat back and counted the commission checks.

If I can do it this way, you can too! But you've got to come together in love and truth seven days a week just like I had to do it with Johnny Langston and Frank Ward. I had to look at Frank Ward as my brother. I had to look at Patsy Ward as my sister. That's the way God wants us to do it.

I remember one night we were flying into Atlanta from Las Vegas. We were having much fun in that plane. A Caucasian brother looked back and asked Frank, "Are you people related to one another?" Frank looked at me and pointed, "That's my brother!"

∾ ∾

.:PAUSE:. Wealth Building Scriptures
Week 5 — My Daily Commitment

1. Sunday – "Ask, and it shall be given you; seek, and ye shall find; knock, and it shall be opened to you:" Matthew 7:7; Luke 11:9.

2. Monday – "Wait on the LORD: be of good courage, and he shall strengthen thine heart: wait, I say on the LORD." Psalm 27:14; "Wait on the LORD, and keep his way, and he shall exalt thee to inherit the land: when the wicked are cut off, thou shalt see *it*." Psalm 37:34.

3. Tuesday – "For ye know the grace of our Lord Jesus Christ, that, though he was rich, yet for your sakes he became poor, that ye through his poverty might be rich." 2 Corinthians 8:9; Matthew 16:24.

4. Wednesday – "And I say unto you, That if two of you shall agree on earth as touching any thing that they shall ask, it shall be done for them of my Father which is in heaven." Matthew 18:19.

5. Thursday - "Greater love hath no man than this, that a man lay down his life for his friends." John 15:13.

6. Friday – "Ask, and it shall be given you; seek, and ye shall find; knock, and it shall be opened to you:" Matthew 7:7; Luke 11:9.

7. Saturday – "My mouth shall speak of wisdom; and the meditation of my heart *shall be* understanding." Psalm 49:3; "The fear of the LORD is the beginning of wisdom: a good understanding have all they that do *his commandments*: his praise endureth for ever. Psalm 111:10 ; "Counsel *is* mine, and sound wisdom: I *am* understanding; I have strength." Proverb 8:14.

8. Bonus - "Cease from anger, and forsake wrath: fret not thyself in any wise to do evil." Psalm 37:8; "A wrathful

109

man stirreth up strife: but *he that is* slow to anger appeaseth strife." <u>Proverb 15:18</u>.

9. Bonus - "Go to the ant, thou sluggard; consider her ways, and be wise:" <u>Proverb 6:6</u>; "The thoughts of the diligent *tend* only to plenteousness; but of every one *that is* hasty only to want." <u>Proverb 21:5</u>; <u>Proverb 12:24</u>; <u>13:4</u>.

10. Bonus - "Behold, the LORD thy God hath set the land before thee: go up *and* possess *it*, as the LORD God of thy fathers hath said unto thee; fear not, neither be discouraged." <u>Deuteronomy 1:21</u>; "And Jesus looking upon them saith, With men it is impossible, but not with God: for with God all things are possible." <u>Mark 10:27</u>; <u>Matthew 19:25</u>; <u>Luke 18:27</u>.

11. Bonus - "And now, Israel, what doth the LORD thy God require of thee, but to fear the LORD thy God, to walk in all his ways, and to love him, and to serve the LORD thy God with all thy heart and with all thy soul, to keep the commandments of the LORD, and his statutes, which I command thee this day for thy good?" <u>Deuteronomy 10:12-13</u>; "And he said to *them* all, If any *man* will come after me, let him deny himself, and take up his cross daily, and follow me." <u>Luke 9:23</u>.

12. Bonus - "And I say unto you, That if two of you shall agree on earth as touching any thing that they shall ask, it shall be done for them of my Father which is in heaven." <u>Matthew 18:19</u>.

13. Bonus - "And he said unto them, Go ye into all the world, and preach the gospel to every creature." <u>Mark 16:15</u>; "the gospel of the kingdom..." <u>Matthew 4:23</u>; <u>9:35</u>; <u>24:14</u>; <u>Mark 1:14</u>.

(Read Wealth Building Scriptures Aloud-3x Daily)

.:PAUSE:. Wealth Building Tips
Week 5 – My Daily Affirmation

1. Sunday - I will look to heaven and speak to Father God.
2. Monday - I will realize that this may not be one of those "immediate" deals; this may be a "wait" deal. I will be patient.
3. Tuesday - I will achieve wealth by following Christ.
4. Wednesday - I will imagine my goals. I will imagine my dreams.
5. Thursday - I will find people in my life who have what I need. I will find people in my life who need what I have.
6. Friday - I will ask and expect it shall be given to me as my actions work towards my goals.
7. Saturday - I will use good insight and proper planning to secure my future.
8. Bonus - I will not make people angry.
9. Bonus - If I do nothing, I will accomplish the same: nothing. I will be a productive contributor to society.
10. Bonus - I will depend on God for encouragement. I will encourage myself, when no one else will. I believe all things are possible for him that believes.
11. Bonus - I will follow God's instructions to the letter. I will never leave anything out. I will obey Father God.
12. Bonus - I will come together with others in Love and Truth.
13. Bonus - I will make God decisions. I will stop being a passive observer in life and be an active participant.

(Read Wealth Building Tips Aloud-3x Daily)

Chapter 6

Make God-Decisions

Using the
P.A.U.S.E. ®
(Practical Application and Use of the Scriptures Everyday)
Wealth Building System

"A double minded man *is* unstable in all his ways."

James 1:8

Doing It God's Way®

Chapter 6

Make God-Decisions

Make a Decision

Don't Turn Back (Genesis 19:26)

In the early seventies at a seminar in Atlanta, Georgia at eight o'clock in the morning, I heard the man considered by many to have been the world's greatest sales trainer, J. Douglas Edwards. I made up my mind that morning that whenever I organized my Real Estate firm, I was going to have him spend time with my sales organization to help organize and boost sales. When I started organizing my Real Estate firm, I started writing him. I wrote him for a period of two years with no reply. Was I disappointed? No. Did I get angry?

No. Did I give up? No. Did I keep trying? Yes. Perseverance is key.

One morning I was on my way to the Real Estate office. I made a decision. I was going to bring in J. Douglas Edwards, the man known in America as the world's greatest sales trainer. When I make a decision, I don't turn back. If you turn back, you're not going to find the success which you seek.

> **When
> We Take Action
> God Takes Action**

Most people wait until they cannot go any further in a situation before they consult God. It is imperative that we consult God first in everything we do. Consulting God first will position you not to make a poor decision. The decision may look like a poor one, but when God is involved it will be one of the best decisions you have made in your life.

When I opened my mouth and asked God to bring in the world's greatest sales trainer, God told me to send his secretary a dozen red roses. J. Douglas Edwards called me the next day.

"Any man that knows how to sell like that," J. Douglas Edwards said, "I've got to come and see what he is about."

The man known by many as the world's greatest sales trainer came to Atlanta, Georgia for AC Brown and his sales team. He brought his son and they stayed an entire week. He put on one of the most elaborate training programs I've ever experienced in my life. *Boy was I in the "big-time" now*, I thought.

J. Douglas Edwards told me that his secretary who had worked for him for twenty-six years had never received any gift like that from anyone requesting an appointment with his firm, nor had anyone in his firm sent her a gift such as this.

He was so impressed that he made me a part of his sales training presentation because I was the first African-American who had hired him. He even had me stand during one of his training seminars. In an audience of about 2,000 attendees, there were only a handful of African-Americans there; AC was one of them. I thought it was all about me and my ability to achieve. It was not. It was and always is about God and His Son Christ Jesus.

I remember during one of his seminars which I attended, J. Douglas Edwards walked over to me, out of a crowd of over 1,000 attendees.

"Young man," he said, "why are you so damn excited?"

I replied, "I don't know why, I just am."

"How many houses do you sell a month?" he asked.

"Ten to fifteen a month."

"I see why you are so damn happy!" J. Douglas Edwards laughed as he delivered these words.

I had to invest over $20,000 in gifts for my sales people to be used during J. Douglas' week of training. The training was so intense we had to close the Real Estate office and go to a hotel. We had "jump" sessions every day. "Jumping" out of our seats with the answers to a myriad of questions. The correct answers were rewarded by the special gifts purchased earlier.

At dinner that evening, I asked J. Douglas Edwards a question. This was the question I asked him. This is the same question you may be asking yourself.

Success is Preparation Connecting with Opportunity

"Why aren't my salespeople consistent in their closing?"

This was his answer. "They don't want what you want." He continued, "They don't want the same thing that you want, Mr. Brown."

I don't buy every answer that comes. I knew from my 48-year track record -- every man and every woman that walks this earth wants exactly what AC Brown wants. The only reason they're not getting it -- they're not "Doing it God's Way." When you do it God's way, no man on earth can compete with you unless they are doing it God's way too.

We've got to understand God owns everything. (Psalm 24) Your day is coming. So you have to prepare for it. Our trip through this land is preparation meeting opportunity. Our successful trip through this land is knowledge prepared to meet opportunity. You have the equipment. Let me show you how to use it. Apply what you learn from this book. When you

118

do it the way I teach you, the bricks automatically fall into place as if magic hands are placing them there. Everything you touch in life will turn to gold.

But God works in due season. If you have prepared under the instructions of the Holy Spirit, it is going to happen. It happened to me before that seminar was over. One day, before the seminar was over it happened just like clockwork.

We were sitting at dinner. The man considered by many as the world's greatest sales trainer was sitting directly across from me. I was sitting across from him and my wife. He looked at my wife and me and his son like he had seen a ghost. His whole personality changed in one split second. Listen to what he said.

"Mr. and Mrs. Brown, this country is in a mess!" He continued, "The reason this country is in a mess is because we have looked all over America trying to find an African-American man to talk about working. He does not exist in this country."

Could it be true, I thought. *He is talking about me.*

He said, "We're not just looking for a good speaker, we are looking for an African-American man that has come up through the rough clay and made millions. Someone who made it on his skills, ability, and hard work."

He is absolutely talking about me now. I know it. I could hardly hold back my excitement. I had to stand up to the man known by many as the world's greatest sales trainer. I looked him dead in his eyes.

119

"You're looking at him," I said to him, "No one has given me anything. I've been into several fields and made millions in each field. My success has been as a result of hard work with God as my guide."

And I sat back down and I listened to what he had to say about that. The man considered by many to be the world's greatest sales trainer laughed.

"Mr. Brown," he responded, "you can do everything I'm looking for. I have observed you since I've been here."

You can imagine my excitement right about now. When you believe that <u>that</u> something is for you, you get all excited. If you expect it with all your heart,

Don't Laugh at God's People

believing without a doubt and it doesn't happen—do not get into a pity-party. You are looking in the face of a blessing delayed; one which is being multiplied on your behalf. Give it time to multiply and get back to you.

"But," he continued, "somewhere down in the grades you missed it."

The man known as the world's greatest salesman did not know I worked nine hours a night putting myself through A & T College. But God knew it. That's the only thing that counts.

I had to stand up again. I said, "I'm going to hire you to get me ready."

"Mr. Brown," he said, "you can't pay me $100,000 a week to get you ready. I make $100,000 a week."

The man considered by many to be the world's greatest sales trainer, who laughed at one of God's children without doing something to help him out, went back to Phoenix, Arizona and died.

Baby-Sitters Cannot Train

I **knew** I had to prepare myself to train people to live life "Doing it God's Way" I put an ad in the Atlanta Constitution before the man known by many as the world's greatest sales trainer landed in Phoenix, Arizona from the seminar he had conducted in Atlanta. When I put that ad in the Atlanta Constitution newspaper, I opened my mouth and I asked God aloud to send me a tough man or lady, a person who would tell it like it is. I did not want a baby-sitter. Baby-sitters cannot train.

Only one man answered the ad, Chuck Hair. This Caucasian brother was the toughest, roughest man I've ever met. He used to call me all kinds of real ugly African-American names. I remember one morning we were in our basement working out and my wife passed through. She heard him shower down one of those real ugly African-American names when he was getting me ready.

After Chuck left she sat me down.

"You mean to tell me," she said, "you're sitting here enjoying every minute of this? And this Caucasian brother is calling you all these different kinds of real ugly African-American names? And furthermore, you're paying him $75 per hour?"

I just looked at her.

"Lea," I said, "I want what that Caucasian brother has to offer."

Chuck Hair came to see me at the end of those two years.

"Mr. Brown" he said, "I'm moving to Boston. My wife and I are getting a divorce."

You've got to understand it this way, when God's ready for a change, He's going to move you and no man can stop Him.

> When God is Ready for a Change He's Going to Move You

"But Mr. Brown," he said, "I want to say something to you before I go."

Listen to this gear shifting. God is telling AC Brown that he has passed the test, but Chuck Hair is saying it. Listen to how Chuck brings it.

"Mr. Brown," he said, "I want to say to you -- you are the toughest man I've ever met. If you sit there and let me call you all those nasty names, you can face any man on this earth."

I'm here to testify to you that <u>the way you go "from rags to riches" ladies and gentlemen – you take what God gave you from birth, what you learn in life, and what you open your mouth and ask God for; mix them together, and you get the</u>

success you seek. You hook the three together. You let no wife, no husband, no mother, no father, no grandparents, no sisters nor brothers, no sisters-in-law nor sons-in-law stop you. This is an individual trip across this land. This is your trip. That is the way you from rags to riches.

Everyone is
Your Classmate
(Luke 6:27-35)

Everyone who needs to be helped is your classmate. God had me give a speech to my twenty-five classmates who helped me get through high school. Remember, I was labeled "just a good old school bus driver." If I can do it this way and get out of the rut and find success with a "C" and "D" transcript from college, that means you can too. I worked nine hours a night putting myself through A & T College. With a work schedule like this I did not have time to study.

When Chuck Hair came to see me, listen how these gears shifted that morning. God is getting ready to make a change.

"Mr. Brown I'm moving to Boston," Chuck said to me, "but I want a few words with you before I go."

That is God shifting those gears, letting me know that I had passed the test. You've got to pass a test before you go to

<u>another level.</u> God is coming on the scene. Listen at this gear shift.

"Mr. Brown you are the toughest man I have ever met. You can make it in front of any audience. I'm here to testify to you."

That was not Chuck Hair talking. That was God sending AC Brown a message that I had passed the test. If I can pass the test, you can too.

That night after Chuck had left, I fell asleep and dreamed that I heard a telephone ringing. In the dream, my wife answered the phone. Guess what she said to me?

"Alonza, guess who is on the telephone? The man known by many as the world's greatest sales trainer, J. Douglas Edwards."

J. Douglas Edwards, the man known by many as the world's greatest sales trainer had been deceased for years. Yes, I answered that telephone. She gave me the phone and guess what J. Douglas said to me?

"I want you to travel this land and tell it like it is."

This was a powerful dream for me and it changed my future. From that moment on I did not have any other choice but to tell it like it is. <u>I've got to tell it like it is and so do you.</u> If I don't tell it like it is, God will come back at me just like a thief in the night. I do not have any other choice but to tell it like it is.

Keys to Your
Personal Success

(Habakkuk 2:2)

Repetition is a spiritual law like the natural law "gravity" that many people ignore, and much like the spiritual law of reciprocity *("what you sow you will reap")* which many people do not know nor understand. When repetition is applied to your goal achievement, you become the winner, tops in your field. I played the Miller Bennett professional sales audiotape for forty-eight years. I just stumbled upon something; it just sounded so good and it worked so well, I continued to use it.

My wife and sons heard it all too often when they rode with me. They got sick and tired of listening to Miller Bennett, over and over each day. A lot of you may know the late Miller Bennett, a world-known professional sales trainer. Many of us will purchase an audiotape or CD and listen to it once.

There is no application of repetition in one listening. Think of a track star, golf pro, or any professional. Ask any of them how often they repeat that which they want to learn. Repeating is a gold mine. Repeat what you want to become over and over until it sticks with you and becomes an integral part of you.

125

.:PAUSE:. **W**ealth **B**uilding **S**criptures
Week 6 — My Daily Commitment

1. Sunday - "My help cometh from the LORD, which made heaven and earth." Psalm 121:2; Luke 11:8.

2. Monday - "Trust in the LORD with all thine heart; and lean not unto thine own understanding. In all thy ways acknowledge him, and he shall direct thy paths." Proverbs 3:5-6; Jeremiah 32:27.

3. Tuesday - "But to us *there is but* one God, the Father, of whom are all things, and we in him; and one Lord Jesus Christ, by whom *are* all things, and we by him." 1 Corinthians 8:6; Psalm 24:1.

4. Wednesday - "Study to shew thyself approved unto God, a workman that needeth not to be ashamed, rightly dividing the word of truth." 2 Timothy 2:15.

5. Thursday - "If any of you lack wisdom, let him ask of God, that giveth to all *men* liberally, and upbraideth not; and it shall be given him." James 1:5; Mark 9:23.

6. Friday - "For by thy words thou shalt be justified, and by thy words thou shalt be condemned." Matthew 12:37.

7. Saturday - "This is my commandment, That ye love one another, as I have loved you." John 15:12; John 15:17.

8. Bonus - "The righteous is more excellent than his neighbor..." Proverb 12:26a; 1 Corinthians 15:57.

(Read Wealth Building Scriptures Aloud-3x Daily)

.:PAUSE:. Wealth Building Tips
Week 6 – My Daily Affirmation

1. Sunday ‐ I will persevere. I will push on, not giving up.

2. Monday ‐ I will consult God first in everything I do. My decision will be the best decision I have made in my life because God is involved.

3. Tuesday ‐ It is not all about me and my ability to achieve. It is about God and His Son Christ Jesus.

4. Wednesday ‐ My successful trip through this land is knowledge preparing to meet opportunity. I will study to prepare to meet opportunity that is coming my way.

5. Thursday ‐ I will take what God gave me from birth, what I learn in life and what I open my mouth and ask God for; and hook them together for my success.

6. Friday ‐ Repeating is a gold mine. I will repeat what I want to be, over and over. I will prepare for what I plan to be until it is an integral part of me. I understand that there is no application of repetition in one listening.

7. Saturday ‐ I realize that everyone who needs help is my classmate. I will help people and learn from people with goals like my own.

8. Bonus - I will apply repetition while executing goal setting. I am a winner, tops in my field.

(Read Wealth Building Tips Aloud-3x Daily)

Chapter 7

Goal Setting

Using the
P.A.U.S.E. ®
(Practical Application and Use of the Scriptures Everyday)
Wealth Building System

"And the LORD answered me, and said, Write the vision, and make it plain upon tables, that he may run that readeth it. For the vision is yet for an appointed time, but at the end it shall speak, and not lie: though it tarry, wait for it; because it will surely come, it will not tarry."

Habakkuk 2:2-3

Doing It God's Way®

Chapter 7

Goal Setting

Keys to
Increased Sales

Leasing Goals. What follows are "tried and true" keys to your personal success if you dare to follow these procedures. Here they are in simple, plain terms. Read carefully. Listen closely.

1) Write down your leasing goals for the month.
2) Write down your leasing goals for the week.
3) Write down your daily leasing goals.
4) Review your goals daily, reading them aloud.
5) Repeat the reading of your goals three times during each reading.

6) Repeat each reading at least three times a day (before or after meals is a good time) and before going to bed at night.

7) Place them on your night table, on your refrigerator, in your walk-in closet, on your wardrobe or on the bathroom mirror. Place them where you will see them everyday; they must be seen.

Here is an example of a typical leasing goal method:

Let's say we have 40 (forty) vacancies in our complex. Since God wants you to prosper and you are going to tithe your 10% or 20% to church and/or charitable organizations. He will help you meet your leasing goals. (Remember, Psalm 24: God owns it all.) So plan to lease all your units—nothing less. That's 40 (forty) units at 10 (ten) per week; that's 2 (two) per day, looking at a 5-day work week.

So your leasing goal would read something like this:

"On or before the last day of the month, I will lease all 40 units in this apartment home complex because my faith is so strong. I can see apartment homes with prospective residents living in them, because I am God's servant as a leasing consultant. I am a steward in God's Kingdom, a servant in His Kingdom and I am serving Him in my job, in my capacity as a leasing consultant. I will lease 10 per week, 20 in 2 weeks, 30 in 3 weeks, 40 in 4 weeks. I have the faith, the knowledge and the know-how. I will get it done."

Place your leasing goal affirmation where you will see it every day: on your wardrobe, in your walk-in closet, on your bathroom mirror or on your refrigerator. This allows your written goals the opportunity to spark your motivation to practice "tried" concepts which work.

The following sections are going to show you how to ensure your goals will be met.

Holy Spirit as a Person

I'**m only hearing** the Pastor talk about the Holy Spirit in the church. What about the Holy Spirit at your job? What about the Holy Spirit when you get in trouble? What about the Holy Spirit in your home? The Holy Spirit is a person. The Holy Spirit has been my teacher for a period of 48 years. The Holy Spirit wants to be your teacher.

If I knew then like I know now, when I was in high school I could have been the best basketball player who ever walked on a court. I could have been the best football player. And I don't care what subjects the teachers taught, I could have run rings around anyone in the classroom.

My experience has been this way when the Holy Spirit teaches a person, no person on earth can compete with him or her unless they are "Doing it God's Way." It's not too late. What am I saying here? It is not too late for every person who is reading this book to allow the Holy Spirit to come into their lives. Allow the Holy Spirit to come into your life and <u>let the Holy Spirit be your teacher</u>. Over my 48-year track record of accomplishment I went into several fields and made millions in each field. If I can do it this way, you can too.

There are a lot of jealous people in this land. If you don't let

> **God Hears
> Every Word
> That Comes
> Out Our Mouths**

the Holy Spirit be your teacher, you can forget you have an interest in this land. The Holy Spirit has an interest in this land. <u>You must have an interest in this land</u> also. Now let me ask you a question. Do you want to increase your wealth? I know everyone raised their hands "yes" in response to this question.

Did you know God knows your thoughts? He knows how you think about this course. He knows your name, your address, and where you live. You can't fool Him.

<u>The only way you can bring the Holy Spirit in to teach you, you've got to be more concerned about God's people than you are about yourself by applying these Scriptures daily in life's small and large situations to allow God's Scriptures to light your daily paths</u>.

God's Attention
Works For You

(Mark 12:21; John 15:13)

Get **God's attention** to work for you. And the way you get God's attention is to be more concerned about His people than you are about yourself. Let me share with you one of the experiences from my 48-year track record.

Walter Jenkins and Sandra Jenkins came to see me. They wanted to sell a home. They didn't want to buy a home. I would have made approximately $8,000 on this sale.

Somewhere in the background I heard these words.

"We are getting a divorce."

I don't care what you do for a living, you're hearing the same thing. But you keep on trying to do business and get that sale. God is hearing every word that is coming out of your mouth. He sees everything you do in life.

I just sat there and stared at Walter Jenkins and Sandra Jenkins.

"Mr. Brown," Mrs. Jenkins said, "why are you staring at us? We just want to sell our home and get on with our separate lives."

I said this laughing after I looked at them for about five minutes. And the reason I laughed was to get them laughing, because for every action there is a reaction.

135

"Mrs. Jenkins and Mr. Jenkins," I said, "I'm trying to figure out where I can go outside and get a big hickory stick and whip y'all all over this office."

When I said this, they thought that was the funniest thing they had ever heard in their lives; they were so astonished, totally surprised by my statement. They had not expected this response. They shared glances with one another and began to laugh.

Move like Jesus When Encountering Disturbing Situations

Now, I had the opportunity to let them know what was going on in their lives. It was nothing but a test; a test for me. The stage was set for a good open discussion.

You're doing the same thing as you travel through this land. Keep on sitting there and not moving in like Christ did. Listen to Christ: *"He who believes on me and the works that I do shall he shall do also. Even greater works than these shall he do because I go unto my Father."*

They reconciled their differences and left laughing, their little girl running behind them. Every time I see this couple, they are thanking me for saving their marriage. If I can do it this way, you can too. It's been 20 years now. Every time I see this couple, they are thanking me for saving their marriage. If I can do it this way, and get the real promises of God that means every person who reads this book can do it too.

God in Us

God is in each one of us. When we see a disturbing situation or even hear about a disturbing situation, we must put forth effort to correct that situation in a godly manner. If we do not put forth an effort to execute God that's inside of each one of us, it's just like God doesn't even exist. That means we have to go out there into the harvest field, just as Christ did when He walked this earth. We have to go out there and help God's people; encourage God's people.

Think Positively Concerning Yourself, Your Family & Your Business

When we see a disturbing situation or even hear about a disturbing situation, and we do not execute the church in us, it's just like that church doesn't even exist. The way we increase our wealth is to execute God within us. My family and I have not had to want for anything since we have been in this world. If I can do it this way that means every person that walks this earth can do it too and receive the real promises of God.

I'm here to testify to you that if you just read your Bible and hear the Word preached and tithe your money, give offerings and if you don't go out there and practice changing tears into joy just like Christ did when He walked this earth, you will never get the real promises of God. I teach you in my books and cassettes and CDs from my 48-year track record, giving you examples, upon examples, and more examples, how to go out there and practice changing tears into joy.

God said He was going to do some new things these last days. And this is one of those new things. Get smart and increase your wealth, but most importantly, live a long, happy and successful life. I'm proud to announce to you I'm 81 years of age. If I can do it this way, you can too.

Church People,
Do What Jesus Did
(John 14:12; Mark 11:23)

I lost my sister and last living brother five days apart. That is when God told me to write this course.

He said, "The world is starving. I want my church people to do what my Son Jesus did when He walked this earth."

Before my brother died, he was real sick. And God asked me to go to see him. As I entered his home, his wife was on the telephone. This was the nature of her conversation.

"Prince didn't eat his breakfast this morning. Prince didn't take his medicine. The minister just left and prayed Prince into heaven."

After that telephone conversation, I pulled Ruth Brown aside.

"When is Prince's funeral going to be?" I asked her.

"What are you talking about?" She asked.

**Do Not Bury Your Husband
While He is Yet Alive**

* * *

**Do Not Bury Your Dreams
While They are Still Alive**

I said to Ruth, "I thought the Bible said through me all things are possible to him that believeth."

Ruth Brown said, "Well."

What else could she say? Then I pulled Ruth Brown and Prince Brown aside and I explained to them what Jesus said. So, at this time I would like to explain the same thing to you.

"He who believes on me and the works that I do shall he do also. Even greater works than these shall he do because I go unto my Father. And whatsoever he shall ask in my name, that will I do, that the Father may be glorified in the Son."

(John 14:12-13; Mark 11:23)

Who is Jesus talking to? Doesn't it sound like Jesus is talking to each one of us? God is inside of each one of us. When we go out there and see a disturbing situation or we hear about a disturbing situation, and we do not put forth an effort to execute God in the situation, it is just like God doesn't even exist.

What did King David do when faced with Goliath? What did the army of Israel do? And what had the army been doing?

139

The *only* way you are going to get the real promises of God, you're going to have to go out there into your community and do the work along with the work you do at your church.

When I left Ruth Brown and Prince Brown, I gave them a warning. And I'm

---

Do not Bury Your Goals by Not Writing Them Down or By Not Working Towards Them

---

warning each one of you who are reading this book, when you go out there and hear about a disturbing situation or even see a disturbing situation -- God saw it and heard it the same time you did. If you don't start doing something about it, encouraging God's people, He'll come back just like a thief in the night. When I left my brother and his wife, my brother came back to a picture of health. That is the good part. The sad part about this experience -- he didn't do anything to help others.

The only thing Ruth Brown and Prince Brown did was sit at home after Sunday morning church service, sit on the porch after dinner and talk about how good the minister preached. They did not execute God in themselves nor go into the harvest field. Don't you make that mistake.

His wife came walking up to me real slowly at the cemetery.

"Lord," she said, "when he fell that morning, I remember what you said – 'It will come back. It will come back just like a thief in the night.' We thought you were joking."

When AC Brown tells you God said it, I'm not joking. I can't afford to joke about something like this, because if I put it as a joke, He'll come back for AC Brown just like a thief in the night. I don't know about you. I want to live a long, happy, and successful life.

฿๏   ๏ʒ

.:PAUSE:. Wealth Building Scriptures
Week 7 — My Daily Commitment

1. Sunday - "Woe unto you, scribes and Pharisees, hypocrites! For ye pray tithe of mint and anise and cumin, and have omitted the weightier *matters* of the law, judgment, mercy, and faith: these ought ye to have done, and not to leave the other undone. Matthew 23:23; Luke 11:42.

2. Monday - "The earth *is* the LORD'S, and the fullness thereof; the world, and they that dwell therein." Psalm 24:1.

3. Tuesday - "And the LORD answered me, and said, Write the vision, and make it plain upon tables, that he may run that readeth it. For the vision is yet for an appointed time, but at the end it shall speak, and not lie: though it tarry, wait for it; because it will surely come, it will not tarry." Habakkuk 2:2-3.

4. Wednesday - "So when even was come, the lord of the vineyard saith unto his steward, Call the labourers, and give them *their* hire, beginning from the last unto the first." Matthew 20:8; "For as the body without the spirit is dead, so faith without works is dead also." James 2:26.

5. Thursday – "But the Comforter, *which is* the Holy Ghost, whom the Father will send in my name, he shall teach you all things, and bring all things to your remembrance, whatsoever I have said unto you." John 14:26.

6. Friday – "And they departed, and went through the towns, preaching the gospel, and healing every where Luke 9:6; 1 Peter 2:21.

7. Saturday – "This is my commandment, That ye love one another, as I have loved you. Greater love hath no man than this, that a man lay down his life for his friends." John 15:12-13; John 13:34; Luke 6:27-35.

8. Bonus - "Ye are of God, little children, and have overcome them: because greater is he that is in you, than he that is in the world." 1 John 4:4; Colossians 1:27.

9. Bonus - "Let them shout for joy, and be glad, that favour my righteous cause: yea, let them say continually, Let the LORD be magnified, which hath pleasure in the prosperity of his servant." Psalm 35:27.

10. Bonus - "A new commandment I give unto you, That ye love one another; as I have loved you, that ye also love one another." John 13:34.

(Read Wealth Building Scriptures Aloud-3x Daily)

.:PAUSE:. **W**ealth **B**uilding **T**ips
Week 7 – My Daily Affirmation

1. Sunday ⁃ God wants me to prosper. I am going to tithe 10% or 20% to my church and/or charitable organization.

2. Monday ⁃ I will remember, Psalm 24: God owns it all. I will make sure my goals are set at 100%. At least 80% of my objectives will be accomplished.

3. Tuesday ⁃ I will visualize my goals: my personal goals, my business goals, my spiritual goals, all my goals.

4. Wednesday ⁃ I am God's servant. I am a steward in God's Kingdom and I am serving Him in my job.

5. Thursday ⁃ I will ask the Holy Spirit to be my teacher.

6. Friday ⁃ I will apply the Scriptures daily in my life to allow God's Scriptures to lighten my small and large situations.

7. Saturday ⁃ I will be more concerned about other people than I am about myself, turning tears into joy by assisting problem situations.

8. Bonus - God is in each one of us. God is within me.

9. Bonus - I will encourage people. I will encourage myself.

10. Bonus - When I see a disturbing situation or even hear about a disturbing situation, I will execute God in me and help someone.

(Read Wealth Building Tips Aloud-3x Daily)

Chapter 8

Words for the Wise

What You Do and Don't Say
Can Help You

Using the
P.A.U.S.E. ®
(Practical Application and Use of the Scriptures Everyday)
Wealth Building System

"For by thy words thou shalt be justified, and by thy words thou shalt be condemned."

Matthew 12:37

Doing It God's Way®

Chapter 8

Words for the Wise

Use Intelligent
Key Statements

Use key words and key statements. When you're working for a prospective resident, the intelligent selection of key words and statements is imperative in establishing and maintaining a positive mental attitude; not only for the prospective resident but for you also. This simple element in making any sale is demonstrated in the examples in this chapter.

It is a simple matter for seasoned professionals who have reached this understanding. I realize which words are the best to use for a particular situation. I then use this knowledge for an expected measured result in conversation and action from my prospective residents.

Here are some prime examples of words and statements that we encounter every day leasing apartment homes.

<u>Never say, "I'm calling to confirm our appointment."</u>

You can accomplish this purpose without using those words, which might insult the prospective resident about keeping his appointment. If he or she already had any doubt about keeping that date, you just offered him or her the perfect way out.

<u>When you call to confirm an appointment to demonstrate an apartment home, use this approach.</u>

"*Mrs. Adams*, this is Joe Jones with Out Front Apartment Community. I have selected the perfect apartment home for you and your family. It has a large separate dining room that will accommodate all of your furniture and a beautiful spacious kitchen with all of the latest conveniences. I'm looking forward to seeing you today at 10:00 a.m. Be sure to bring the children along too."

<u>Also ask to speak to the spouse and address his interests.</u>

"*Mr. Adams*, I've selected the perfect apartment home for you and your family. It has a large modern kitchen that your wife wanted and a wonderful yard for children. I'm looking forward to seeing you and Mrs. Adams and the children today at 10:00 a.m. sharp. You're going to just love this apartment home. Keep in mind that your wife is an important part of this decision."

As the leasing agent, <u>get permission from the husband to speak to the wife</u> concerning apartment leasing issues. This is done to get and keep them both involved. This is very important in leasing. Both the husband and wife must know that they both are an important part of making the leasing decision. Ensure to talk to both spouses, looking them both in the eyes when leasing them their new apartment home.

Children Will Help Mom and Dad Close the Transaction

ॐ ॐ

Walk-Ins

Walk-ins. For prospective residents who do not have an appointment, <u>treat them just like they have an appointment</u>. Do not hesitate. Do not disrespect them in any way. Go right into leasing the apartment home as if they had made an appointment. You can lead with a statement like this:

"<u>I have some really nice apartments which you will just love</u>."

At this point, I would have the walk-ins sit down around my desk. And when they sit down, as the leasing consultant, I would figure out which person in their group is really in charge. <u>The one who asks the most questions and seems to be</u>

149

the most concerned is probably the one in charge. I would not hesitate as they are taking their seats to begin asking them questions.

Answers. And once I get their answers, I would analyze their answers and write them down; doing my very best to familiarize myself with the answers which they gave me so if I have to refer back to the answers again, I will be familiar with them.

Be very brief and precise and to the point and ask those questions in a very friendly voice. Remember, to smile as you talk. Practice at this point, putting humor in your questions to get them laughing. Laughing does create leases. Laughter creates sales in any field.

Questions. Once I field their questions, I analyze their questions and write them down; doing my very best to familiarize myself with the questions which they ask me so if I have to refer back to the questions again, I will be familiar with them.

Be very brief and precise and to the point and answer those questions in a friendly voice. Remember, to smile as you talk. Practice at this point, putting humor in your answers to get them laughing. Laughing does create leases. Laughter creates sales in any field.

I would like to recommend at this point, that if you do not have a sense of humor, go and purchase some clean joke books. While sitting at your desk between appointments and your other duties, practice the jokes. It makes a difference to your livelihood.

Father God has given everyone on this planet the ability to laugh. People tend not to <u>use common human denominators like laughter</u>.

This one move can help you keep your leasing job. If that happens (you losing your job) it will only be your fault because you did not use what you just read. It is not that we do not have customers, what it boils down to is: we do not have friendly leasing people who want to be friendly helping God's people.

꿍   꿍

Use Key Statements
and Key Words

* ❖ Before demonstrating an apartment home, never say:
  * • "Let us go out and look."
  * • Instead say: "<u>Let us go out and _select_</u>."

If you say look, that is exactly what a prospective resident is going to do. Look.

❖ <u>*Select*</u> is what you really want them to do, isn't it? Or you may say it this way:

- "When you are getting ready to go out to <u>select</u>, Mr. and Mrs. Adams..."

You want to say to them very positively; with a winning smile displayed on your face.

"Now <u>get ready</u> to move."

Make sure both parties hear this when they return from viewing the apartments. What happens next is you go ahead and fill out the paperwork and ask them for the money. You do not hesitate at this point.

Article written by AC Brown for Real Estate Today Magazine when He was selling houses at 17%.

❖ Never say to other leasing consultants in front of any prospective residents:

- "I'm going to show this apartment home."
- Instead say: "<u>I am going to lease this apartment home today</u>."

Use only positive, direct and expectant statements. Remember this always, <u>you must program yourself to close</u> as a leasing consultant. We talk about programming the computer, what about programming prospective residents and ourselves?

What I am really saying is we have to program ourselves to close a prospective resident on a lease, because that is the only reason they came in the first place. They wanted some place to stay and they have come to you. Just think for a moment.

<u>There are hundreds of apartment communities in this city, and they came to you.</u>

- ❖ If they came to you they must need your help. Say to them:
  - "We will arrange your financing for approval."
  - Not: "We want to order a credit report."

Often the word *"credit"* reminds prospective residents of past financial experiences that they think may cause problems. To avoid facing reality, they will give excuses for not leasing. In all actuality, these financial experiences may not adversely hurt the transaction at all.

- ❖ So sow service and harvest money.
  Never ask:
  - "Would you like to lease this apartment home today?" People may think that they have bought too much already.

- Ask instead, "Would you like an <u>opportunity</u> to lease this apartment home today?"

❖ When you're talking about the rental rate, leave off thousands in dollars. Try saying it this way.
  - "Mr. Adams, the rental rate is 4." He still understands you, but "4" sounds less intimidating than "dollars"; $400 or $4,000.

❖ Never say the word *"sorry."* This is a negative approach. Example:
  - "I'm sorry this apartment is not available."
  - "I'm sorry that you have to walk up this steep slope."

Prospective residents may begin to think, *"Perhaps I will be sorry."*

Better approaches are:
  - "We have the perfect apartment home for you." Or:
  - "You can see how our apartment homes are integrated into the surrounding nature." Or:
  - "You'll be proud of yourself for selecting one of our apartment homes."

ଃୠ   ଓୡ

Use Intelligent
Key Words

❖ Say "agreement" not lease. Prospective residents want to feel that they are entering freely into a real estate transaction, not that they are obligated against their will.

❖ Never use the words "qualify" and "afford." These are words to use with other leasing consultants. These words can make prospective residents defensive and perhaps apprehensive. They do not want you to tell them what they can and cannot afford. Your questions will determine their level of affordability.

❖ Say, "transaction" not "deal." The word deal has a suspicious tone to it. Transaction has a more legitimate connotation.

❖ Say, "I congratulate you," more often than "thank you." Saying "thank you" implies that the prospective resident has done something for you. "I congratulate you" confirms the fact that they have made the right decision for themselves.

❖ Remember this always. When leasing an apartment home, use colorful descriptive glamorous words.

Can you imagine a sandwich made with thin-sliced, sweet, Danish ham, aged Swiss cheese, fresh crisp iceberg lettuce and firm sliced ripe tomatoes on freshly baked cracked wheat bread?

Doesn't that sound a lot more appetizing than ham and cheese on whole wheat? In the same manner, you can make that ham and cheese product called apartment home leasing sound a lot more appetizing to new prospective residents. Make using colorful, glamorous words a habit so they become an integral part of your vocabulary.

℘   ℘

Show One Product
Sell One Product

Show one product, sell one product. Remember this always when demonstrating apartment homes: prospective residents came to your apartment community office and asked for only one apartment home. He or she did not ask for two or three. Only one.

You may look at this as poor teaching, but this one thing can make you or break you, because the prospective resident hears every word out of your mouth. And once it is released, you cannot go back and get it. It took me twenty-one years to exercise the courage to execute this sales approach.

When they ask for one, you only show them one. Not two, not three, not four, not five, or you have messed up your process. The process being—you must determine which apartment home is best for them before you leave the leasing office.

የ፝   ርፃ

Do it this way. You are leaving the office with the couple, when you get about half-way across the yard, you stop. You ask them.

"Don't you just love this apartment home community?"

Head towards the apartment home to which you were en route.

When you open that door and they enter their new apartment home, you stop in the middle of the floor and ask them.

"Don't you just love this apartment home?"

Their response and action will tell you what to do next.

"Yes, Mrs. Leasing Consultant, I love this apartment home."

Then you go right back to the office and write up that agreement.

This is apartment leasing at its highest.

If they ask for one-bedroom, two-bedroom, or three-bedroom apartment homes, use the same procedure. I do not care how tough the market gets.

Do this: it took me years to learn it. This procedure works, but you have to practice and believe it will work.

℘   ℩

The Professional Doctor's Office

I want you to picture the professional doctor's office. He has a waiting room filled with people who are waiting to see him. Picture that. Now you imagine your waiting room filled with waiting customers with pockets filled with money or credit cards. Imagine people wanting your services as the people sitting waiting in the professional doctor's office.

When the professional doctor examines his patient, runs tests and the test results come back, he says to his patient.

"Mrs. Adams, I have completed the test and I discovered that you need an operation."

158

The professional doctor would never say to Mrs. Adams:

"Now before I operate, here are two doctor's business cards and they are in the same profession that I'm in. I would like you to go and let them run tests, then you make a decision on which doctor you want to use."

You could not pay this doctor with that white coat on to do it that way. The professional doctor makes decisions for his patients. What about the professional apartment home leasing consultant?

Your prospective residents want you to make decisions for them. They need your expertise. If you have done your job well, they will respect your opinion. Start leasing and selling this way. Practice this approach and it will surely work for you.

ဆ　　ဢ

The Professional Doctor's Approach - Example

THE PROFESSIONAL DOCTOR'S APPROACH

a. You sit on the edge of your chair.

b. You listen with a sparkle in your eye and love every word your prospective resident is saying.

c. You've got to know your inventory. <u>This is very important.</u> You've got to love your job as a leasing consultant.

d. When that light bulb comes on in your imagination and you have determined the right apartment for your prospective residents, you snap your fingers – and say, "I've got it." And you do it excitedly with energy and vigor when plucking your fingers—give your fingers some drama. "Snap."

e. And you talk about that one apartment home that you have selected for them <u>just like you have discovered America for your prospective residents.</u> Remember, your new residents could be living in their new apartment home for the next ten years.

If you have guts enough to lease this way, your leasing volume will skyrocket. You talk about that one apartment
160

home just like you have discovered America for them, and you have. Now, you as a professional leasing consultant will have more prospective residents than you'll know what to do with. You'll be just like the professional doctor.

He makes decisions for his patients. Practice this technique to perfection so it is second nature to you; so it feels, looks, and sounds natural.

Remember this always—save time and get your job done the professional doctor's way, keeping your mind on your prospective residents.

Your job and livelihood is to love to serve people. As the professional leasing consultant remember you are leasing your new prospective residents their new homes. Start practicing the PAUSE Wealth Building System Scriptures and Tips and you will lease more apartment homes than you can imagine.

ဆာ   ဏ

.:PAUSE:. Wealth Building Scriptures
Week 8 — My Daily Commitment

1. Sunday – "For by thy words thou shalt be justified, and by thy words thou shalt be condemned." <u>Matthew 12:37</u>.

2. Monday – "And we know that all things work together for good to them that love God, to them who are the called according to *his* purpose." <u>Romans 8:28</u>.

3. Tuesday – "So *shall* the knowledge of wisdom *be* unto thy soul: when thou hast found <u>it</u>, then there shall be a reward, and thy expectation shall not be cut off." <u>Proverb 24:14</u>.

4. Wednesday – "...I said, I will take heed to my ways, that I sin not with my tongue: I will keep my mouth with a bridle, while the wicked is before me." <u>Psalm 39:1</u>; <u>James 1:26</u>; "*He that is* slow to anger *is* better than the mighty; and he that ruleth his spirit than he that taketh a city." <u>Proverb 16:32</u>; <u>Proverb 15:18</u>.

5. Thursday – "A feast is made for laughter, and wine maketh merry: but money answereth all *things*." <u>Ecclesiastes 10:19</u>. "Mercy and truth are met together; righteousness and peace have kissed *each other*." <u>Psalm 85:10</u>.

6. Friday – "I returned, and saw under the sun, that the race *is* not to the swift, nor the battle to the strong, neither yet bread to the wise, nor yet riches to men of understanding, nor yet favour to men of skill; but time and chance happeneth to them all." Ecclesiastes 9:11.

7. Saturday - "But let your communications be, Yea, yea; Nay, nay: for whatsoever is more than these cometh of evil." Matthew 5:37; "But I say unto you, Love your enemies, bless them that curse you, do good to them that hate you, and pray for them which despitefully use you, and persecute you;" Matthew 5:44.

8. Bonus - "Then Jesus beholding him loved him, and said unto him, One thing thou lackest: go thy way, sell whatsoever thou hast, and give to the poor, and thou shalt have treasure in heaven: and come, take up the cross, and follow me." Mark 10:21; Fulfil ye my joy, that ye be likeminded, having the same love, *being* of one accord, of one mind." Philippians 2:2.

9. Bonus - "Now the God of hope fill you with all joy and peace in believing, that ye may abound in hope, through the power of the Holy Ghost." Romans 15:13; "Serve the LORD with gladness: come before his presence with singing." Psalm 100.2.

10. Bonus - "But above all things, my brethren, swear not, neither by heaven, neither by the earth, neither by any other oath: but let your yea be yea; and *your* nay, nay; lest ye fall into condemnation." James 5:12.

11. Bonus – "And he shall be like a tree planted by the rivers of water, that bringeth forth his fruit in his season; his leaf also shall not wither; and whatsoever he doeth shall prosper." Psalm 1:3.

(Read Wealth Building Scriptures Aloud-3x Daily)

.:P.A.U.S.E:. Wealth Building Tips
Week 8 – My Daily Affirmation

1. Sunday - I will use positive words and practice using them.
2. Monday - I will select and use intelligent key words and intelligent statements. This will help me establish and maintain a positive mental attitude.
3. Tuesday - I will use words in conversation to get an expected result. I will direct the outcome of my conversations.
4. Wednesday - In conversation, I will be brief, precise and to the point, asking questions in a very friendly voice; remembering to smile as I talk.
5. Thursday - I will use common human denominators like laughter to establish and re-establish relationships.
6. Friday - I will program myself to close during all conversations.
7. Saturday - I will not be negative in any of my conversations. I will always have a positive expectant attitude.
8. Bonus - I will focus on demonstrating one product and selling one product at a time.
9. Bonus - I will be excited about what I am selling, my job, my church, my family. I realize excitement nurtures interest.
10. Bonus - I will make decisions for those who I want to influence.
11. Bonus - My production will skyrocket. I will lease many apartment homes.

(Read Wealth Building Tips Aloud-3x Daily)

Chapter 9

The Professional Sales Approach

Using the
P.A.U.S.E. ®
(Practical Application and Use of the Scriptures Everyday)
Wealth Building System

Whatever You Have Is Nothing
If You Do Not Put It Into Action

Doing It God's Way®

Chapter 9

The Professional
Sales Approach

God Taught Me
to Sell Eggs

The egg story. Five summers ago, I was visiting my wife's hometown in Wilson, North Carolina. I had been driving all day when we arrived in rural Wilson. The late Mrs. Ruffin, my wife's mother, 90 years of age, came to me.

"Brown, take me to Wilson. I have 48 dozen eggs to take up there and some collard greens."

The way she said it, I was under the impression that these eggs were already sold and we were only making a delivery. It was just a matter of taking Mrs. Ruffin up there and unloading those eggs and collard greens. That is what I thought.

When we arrived in Wilson, I noticed Mrs. Ruffin was going from door to door trying to sell the 48 dozen eggs and those collard greens. Wait a minute! I had to do something. I had been driving all day and I was tired and sleepy. This is what I did because I had never sold eggs before.

I opened my mouth and I asked God to teach me how to sell those eggs. If I can do it this way, you can too while leasing apartment homes. It's in the Bible and this is the way it is worded. *"Ask and it shall be given you. Seek and ye shall find. Knock and it shall be opened unto you. For anyone that asketh, receiveth, he that seeketh findeth, and to him that knocketh, it shall be opened."*

All I had to do was open my mouth and ask God to teach me how to sell these eggs. If I can ask Him to teach me how to sell eggs, you can ask Him to teach you how to lease apartment homes. Ask Him to teach you how to lease those apartment homes.

I do not start a new job or start a new business, or change church membership unless I open my mouth and ask God. If you do it this way, no man on earth can compete with you unless he is "Doing it God's Way."

℘   ℘

Specialize
In the Five B's

Before we can do it God's way, when leasing apartment homes or no matter what business you are in, you must specialize in the five B's.

* ❖ **Be professional, dress appropriately.**
  You must look the part.
* ❖ **Be enthusiastic.** God is enthusiastic.
* ❖ **Be busy.**
  Act as if you have things to do and places to go, because you do.
* ❖ **Believe in your product.**
  Believe in the product's benefits.
* ❖ **Be knowledgeable about your product.**
  Know your product. Product knowledge must be presented as a benefit to your prospective resident.

No matter what business you are in, no matter what job you are working, as you work the five B's you have got to say the correct words in the correct tones to be highly effective. Say something that will make them stop and listen to what you have to say. Say something which is beneficial to them.

Fresh Country Eggs

God planted these words into my subconscious mind: *"fresh country eggs."* <u>I have disciplined myself to keep my mind on God at all times and my ears listening for God</u>. Those words rose to my conscious mind.

Now, when I heard those words – "fresh country eggs." I knew how to fill in the blanks. I reached in the automobile. I got eight crates of eggs and I put them under my arm and

CROWDS

CREATE

SALES

some collard greens, and started walking the streets yelling.

"Frr-eessh country eggs, frr-eessh country eggs."

Notice the word *"fresh."* I used that word with emotion. I painted a picture of my eggs being fresh. If I can do it this way, you can too.

Children playing football in the street stopped their game, ran into their homes to bring their mothers out to buy my fresh country eggs. The beauty of the whole thing is that they came out. Now when these mothers came out to buy my fresh country eggs, I asked them.

"Would you like <u>two</u> or <u>three</u> dozen of eggs?"

Notice I did not ask how many dozens they wanted. I asked them if they wanted two or three dozen. Most mothers requested three dozen. <u>Never forget the power of suggestion.</u>

170

Housewives came in large numbers. Don't ever forget this – <u>excitement and crowds do create sales</u>.

There was a man crossing the intersection on a bicycle. He heard me yelling, "fresh country eggs." He made a U-turn and came back and bought a dozen eggs. There was also a man at the top of a 50-foot power pole. He stopped his repair work, climbed down and bought two dozen eggs.

That's not the end of the story. The end of this story goes like this. There was also a man directly across the street in front of where I was selling all these eggs. He was selling eggs too. He came over, rushing over to me.

"How much are you getting for your eggs?" He asked.

And you know what he discovered? He discovered that I was getting a better price than he was getting for his eggs. His eggs were cheaper, but they were not selling. I believe today, if I had just asked him to buy some of my eggs, he would have bought some of my eggs although he was selling eggs too.

It's right there in the Bible, *"ask and it shall be given you, seek and ye shall find, knock and it shall be opened unto you. For everyone that asketh, receiveth, he that seeketh, findeth, and to him that knocketh, it shall be opened."*

If I can learn how to sell eggs this quickly, you can learn how to lease apartments quickly also. That's "Doing it God's Way." Remember this always -- God owns it all, and without Him, you and I cannot do anything.

The Doctor's Professional Approach

Let me ask you a question. Have you ever seen a boy flying a kite? That kite is way up in the air. That boy is not up there with that kite. That boy is on the ground holding a string, but that boy is still controlling that kite. Leasing consultant, apartment managers, do you understand you can lease apartments that way?

You do not have to go out there with the prospective residents always. You can stay in your office and be fresh to serve, shake hands, and think how to close. You will lease more apartments if you are not stressed out. Successful apartment home leasing is successful selling at its best.

That boy is not up there flying that kite. He is on the ground. The wind is holding that kite up. We all know that God controls the wind just as He helps us control our words, our actions and our enthusiasm.

Effective Telephone Conversation. When you're on your telephone in your office, always program your prospects to come to your office at a particular day and time. You program them to be in your office at 10 o'clock Thursday morning.

Say: *"I'll be here at 10 o'clock Thursday morning waiting on you and Mr. Nash."*

And find out if they have children. Ask them to bring the children along. Ask them to *"bring John"* with them, if that's the little boy. <u>Children help Mom and Pop close</u>. Pick up little John—but do not drop him.

We talk about programming the computer, what about programming the prospective residents? Programming begins with your telephone conversation. <u>You've got to have the words and you've got to have them right</u>. This is what you say.

"Mrs. Nash get ready to move."

She'll never forget those words as long as she lives – "get ready to move." The fact that she has called is proof that she wants to move.

You're fresh. You can stay in your office smiling, serving coffee, shaking hands; watching your prospective residents drive up to your office. This is powerful selling. Go out there and greet them. Open car doors, smiling, shaking hands; not a vice grip however. When they drive up to your apartment home leasing office, <u>walk out to greet them</u>. Open the car doors for the driver. Open the passenger door, the back door and walk around the car to open the door on the other side. Before they come into your office, say.

"Come into my office and get ready to move."

I want you to understand something. Do you realize you are closing that lease to that apartment home when you do these things up front? This procedure works whether you are selling apartment homes, automobiles, Real Estate, or whatever you do for a living.

You feel good. You haven't been out there walking in the sun from apartment to apartment. Ask yourself this question. What do you think are the chances of you leasing five, six, seven, and eight and ten apartment homes per day? Many readers of this book are doing this now. So can you!

I head towards my office and they follow me. Remember, have them sit at your desk and then you take charge. The way to start this approach is important.

Use the Correct Words in the Correct Tones to Persuade People

Sit on the edge of your chair. Take your chair from behind your desk and sit beside your perspective resident. In order to lease this way, you have to change the way you execute your professional courtesy.

The people coming to lease your apartment homes are associating you with the potential service and accommodations which they are to receive while living in your apartment home community. People evaluate you, "size you up" beginning with their first contact with you.

Let me restate again this point of importance: you have to know your inventory. Know what is available. Then you learn your new prospective residents by asking questions. Listen and observe. As you ask key questions about their wants and needs you are mentally selecting the right apartment for them. Listen and observe.

You may have 50 vacancies, but you are only going to lease one apartment home to them. I listen to them talk about the apartment they want. Then snap your fingers and say:

"I have it!"

Selling is acting at its highest. Acting is the highest form of selling. Describe their apartment home to them by painting word pictures of the kitchen and the beautiful hardwood floors. Use descriptive, glamorous words. Always have a list of these descriptive phrases embedded in your presentation. Do not procrastinate; send them out with great anticipation. Remember, keep blinds down in apartment homes which are vacant. There is no need to advertise vacancies with big blank open windows.

Walk out in front of the office and point in the direction, which you want them to go. When they return to your office, they will be ready to complete their paper work and leave a deposit. They will tell you they want to do this. Professional selling is getting your prospects to do what you want them to do without confusing or irritating them.

In larger apartment home communities, a small map may be necessary. Before they leave you though, make sure everyone involved hear these words calling their names.

"Mr. and Mrs. Adams, get ready to move."

You talk about programming our computers, what about our prospective residents?

You tell them:

"I want you to <u>get ready to move</u>. Mr. and Mrs. Adams when you go out there, make sure in your mind you place your furniture like you want it to be. I will be here waiting for you when you return. When you get out there, you've got your cell phone with you, give me a call and let me know to get your paperwork ready so you can move."

> Smile
> and Be
> Very Friendly

When I look out my real estate office window and I see my customers coming back, I don't sit in that office. I go out there and I meet them and I'm smiling and shaking hands. They're grinning and I'm grinning.

<u>You couldn't pay me to ask them if they want it</u>. <u>You could not pay me to ask them what they think</u>. <u>You could not pay me to ask them if they want to look at some more</u>.

The first question I ask when they sit down in my office is to give me the name in which you want to put on the paperwork. If they give me that name, what are they really telling AC Brown? I want an apartment home. I don't ask them should I write it up. When they give me that name, what are they telling me? I want an apartment home. I don't have to ask them if it is okay to write up the agreement. They have given me that name. All I have to do is turn it around and ask them to okay it.

As leasing consultants, if we do not move in this direction at this point, we will not have anyone to demonstrate apartment homes to tomorrow nor the next day nor the next.

This is the time <u>you ask them for five referrals before they get what they want</u>. You'll be surprised how this works.

Five-Referral Procedure

Referrals. The egg story is when I discovered what to do to create sales. The Holy Spirit has been my teacher for a period of 48 years. <u>The Holy Spirit wants to be your teacher</u>. The Holy Spirit wants me to teach you how to sell, remembering <u>everyone is always selling something</u>. The Holy Spirit wants me to teach you how to lease apartment homes; how to keep your apartment community filled. I challenge any man, any woman in the apartment home leasing business to surrender to God and let the Holy Spirit be your teacher. Don't just be out there doing something, doing anything. Do everything through God.

Now it is time to get business for weeks to come by getting referrals. The chief way I sold so many houses over the years was by using *referrals — the five referral procedure*. I always ask God to help my clients give me referrals.

When you ask for those five referrals, this is the way you do it. Ask them to give you the names and phone numbers of five families needing to move. When you ask your prospective residents, you lower your voice like you do not want the people in the next room to hear what you're saying. You act as though you do not want anyone else to hear you. Understand me, using these procedures and approaches takes practice. You've got to practice them.

At the same time when you ask them, your ink pen goes in a writing position because every action creates a reaction. You're not smiling now. Do not smile, be serious. Have a sincere look on your face. This is serious business because prospecting these clients will give you your new business.

"Ask and it shall be given you. Everyone that asketh, receiveth." If this was not real, God would not have put it in the Bible in several places. (Matthew 7:7; Luke 11:9; John 15:7: John 15:16; John 16:23)

When the interest rates were 17%, I used the *referral procedure* and carried several buyers and sellers to Attorney Richard Raymer's office in one day and closed every one of them. All of these customers were referrals.

We've got to look at it this way. If it were not for God, you and I would not even be here. We are here for a purpose. We've got to bring that professional decision through God. If we don't do it, it will cost us dearly.

God owns it all – the shrubs, the trees, the flowers, the apartment home leasing companies, the apartment home customers, the apartment home sellers and the prospective residents, and the apartment home leasing professionals, and the apartment home communities.

ॐ   ॐ

.:PAUSE:. Wealth Building Scriptures
Week 9 — My Daily Commitment

1. Sunday — "I beseech you therefore, brethren, by the mercies of God, that ye present your bodies a living sacrifice, holy, acceptable unto God, *which is* your reasonable service." Romans 12:1; Matthew 25:14-30.

2. Monday – "Ask, and it shall be given you; seek, and ye shall find; knock, and it shall be opened to you:" Matthew 7:7; Luke 11:9.

3. Tuesday - "He that hath knowledge spareth his words: and a man of understanding is of an excellent spirit." Proverb 17:27; Proverb 8:6.

4. Wednesday – "Then was our mouth filled with laughter, and our tongue with singing: then said they among the heathen, The LORD hath done great things for them." Psalm 126:2; Psalm 37:30.

5. Thursday – "Watch ye therefore, and pray always, that ye may be accounted worthy to escape all these things that shall come to pass, and to stand before the Son of man." Luke 21:36; Luke 18:1, Psalm 37:30.

6. Friday – "But let all those that put their trust in thee rejoice: let them ever shout for joy, because thou defendest them: let them also that love thy name be joyful in thee." Psalm 5:11; James 1:2.

7. Saturday – "Moreover the profit of the earth is for all: the king *himself* is served by the field." Ecclesiastes 5:9.

8. Bonus – "But Jesus said, Suffer little children, and forbid them not, to come unto me: for of such is the kingdom of heaven." Matthew 19:14; Mark 10:14, Luke 18:16.

9. Bonus – "Finally, *be ye* all of one mind, having compassion one of another, love as brethren, *be* pitiful, be courteous: not rendering evil for evil, or railing for railing: but contrariwise blessing; knowing that ye are thereunto called, that ye should inherit a blessing." 1 Peter 3:8-9.

10. Bonus – "But I say unto you, Love your enemies, bless them that curse you, do good to them that hate you, and pray for them which despitefully use you, and persecute you;" Matthew 5:44; Proverb 18:24.

11. "Then shall he answer them, saying, Verily I say unto you, Inasmuch as ye did *it* not to one of the least of these, ye did *it* not to me." Matthew 25:45; Matthew 25:31-46.

(Read Wealth Building Scriptures Aloud-3x Daily)

.:PAUSE:. Wealth Building Tips
Week 9 – My Daily Affirmation

1. Sunday - What I have is like nothing if I do not put it into action. I will put my talents into action for God.
2. Monday - I will ask God for what I desire. I will seek it and knock on doors to find it; and thank God for it before I have it.
3. Tuesday – I will learn and practice the five B's. I will be the best at what I am doing.
4. Wednesday – I will say something that will make potential new customers stop and listen.
5. Thursday – I will discipline myself to keep God on my mind at all times. I will be mindful of God in all things.
6. Friday – My excitement about life, myself, family, church and business will increase my sales.
7. Saturday – I will know my inventory so I can match the inventory with its new owner.
8. Bonus - I will allow children to help mom and pop close.
9. Bonus - I will improve the way I execute professional courtesy, associating myself with the products, services and / or accommodations I sell.
10. Bonus - I will practice being friendly, smiling as I speak; realizing success in selling requires being a good actor.
11. Bonus - I will ask customers, clients, members, and prospects for five referrals.
12. Bonus - I will find a need that needs filling and fill it. I am here with a purpose.

(Read Wealth Building Tips Aloud-3x Daily)

Chapter 10

Professional
Apartment Leasing

Using the
P.A.U.S.E.®
(Practical Application and Use of the Scriptures Everyday)
Wealth Building System

"Two are better than one; because they have a good reward for
their labour."

Ecclesiastes 4:9

Doing It God's Way®

Chapter 10

Professional
Apartment Leasing

Get Referrals

Now **how are we** going to get more people? You get your referrals before that prospective resident gets what he or she wants, which is an apartment home. Notice I have not asked them for any money. I'm going to bring that up after I get my <u>five referrals</u>.

You say to them –

"Mr. and Mrs. Nash, when I take your application to my manager, I want to make sure that the manager knows you have referred five more people that want an apartment home out here. And when I have a vacancy, I'm going to call these people and tell them you referred me to them and that you

would like for them to move out here with you. Give me five more people that are interested in getting an apartment home."

Why did I go that way? They told me they liked what they saw when they told me that name that they wanted to put the lease in. When I ask them for those five referrals, I ask them with the tone of voice just like I don't want the people in the next room to hear what I'm saying. <u>Acting is a part of leasing</u>. And this requires practice.

While selling Real Estate, I sold 10 to 15 homes a month, even when the interest rate was 17%. How did I do it? Let me tell you how. <u>I practiced getting referrals</u>. I would walk up to a 14-year-old just as big as time; just as quickly as I would an adult.

"Have you ever thought about owning your own home?"

I got a sale and wasn't even expecting it. When you practice this way, this thing gets real. She twisted around.

"You know I'm too young to own my own home."

She thought for a few seconds, then she said.

"I heard my mother and father talking about it the other day."

I pulled my little book out of my pocket and I got a sale and wasn't even expecting it because I had been practicing. This is the way you do it; you practice. <u>You practice until you perfect your approaches and your closes</u>. You'll lease more apartments than you ever thought possible when you practice your sales techniques and when you use the *"Wealth Building*

Scriptures and Tips" at the end of each chapter. You can't just think about this thing when you walk on a job in the morning. This is your livelihood. <u>Sow service</u> and lease apartment homes. This is the way you do it.

You ask your prospective residents in a tone of voice like you don't want the people in the next room to hear what you are saying. At the same time, your ink pen goes in a writing position. Why? Because <u>for every action there is a reaction</u>. You are thinking and believing, knowing they're going to give you five referrals. Now you may not get but two, but that's better than what you had. Just keep doing it and the more you do it this way, the more people are going to be sitting out there in your reception room because of *the five-referral program.*

Oh, this is a beautiful world we're living in. The only thing wrong with this world is we are not using the road map called the Bible to travel by. Do it the way I teach you. Your prospective residents will qualify people for you. <u>Your current residents will qualify people for you.</u>

When you ask them for those five referrals, remember to ask them to give you the names of <u>people who trust them, who they trust, who believe them, who believes in them, or who will do what they ask them to do; and people who want something out of life</u>. You will be surprised at how high your sales volume goes. You are looking for good people who can afford your product.

You'll make more sales than you'll know what to do with. And you're in the selling profession. I do not care if you are leasing apartment homes, selling automobiles, or Real Estate that's the way you do it. You keep going over the sales techniques in this book. Keep going over it until you perfect it. <u>Fit it into your personality</u>. Let it become a part of you.

This is the way you sell.

"Mrs. Adams, tomorrow I'm going to present your application to my manager. And I want my manager to know that you have <u>referred five prospective residents</u> who want the same thing you want. I'm going to be looking at my manager eyeball to eyeball when I tell him this."

This is how you get so many people to desire to live at your apartment home community, to love living there and to want to get there friends and relatives to live there too.

꿍 ꐑ

Remember
This Close

Remember this close. Then I say to them, "It is not easy to get approved for an apartment these days, so we use every technique available."

It is important to use the correct words in the correct tones to persuade people to do what you want them to do. You'll be surprised at how that can run prospective residents off if you don't do it this way. Tell the prospective resident that you will tell your manager when you sit down with him that the prospective resident has referred five people that are looking for an apartment home community.

Say: "Who do you know that you think would like to move into this community, although I do not have any vacancies right now. I will put them on my reserve list and when a vacancy comes up I will let them know."

And when you say this to them, make sure you are saying it with a low tone of voice, but clear enough for them to understand it, say it to them as though you do not want the people in the next room to hear what we are saying. You are sitting on the tip of your chair when you are talking to them. Boy that will sell.

Ask them to give you the names in order of the priority that they want to do business. Only take five. Just take five. Say:

"Give me their names and their telephone numbers and tell them I will be calling."

When you ask them for the referrals pull out your pen and get ready to write. <u>For every action there is a reaction. When you get your pen ready to write they will get their mouth ready to talk.</u>

Remember this always, you use this procedure, when they say to you as the leasing consultant, I just love that apartment and I want it. This is when you go into the five referrals. You use this before they get what they want. If you come back later, it is too late; the ball game is over. This is what they are going to tell you.

For Every Action

There is a Reaction

"If I think about someone, I will be calling you."

They will never call you—never. I hate to say it but we are in a selfish world and if you do not get those referrals now, you can forget them.

To get your show on the road as a professional leasing consultant <u>all you need is one prospective resident who is ready, willing, and able and who wants to move into your apartment community or a resident who is already there</u>. You have to practice this technique and fit it into your personality before it will work professionally.

As a leasing professional, you are in control. When you're sitting in your office as a leasing consultant and prospective residents are steadily coming in your office and they are asking for you, you're in control. You're in the apartment home leasing business. If they hear that people are coming in that apartment office asking for you, you're in control. Or if they enter the reception room and see people sitting out there waiting on you, you as a professional leasing consultant, you are in charge and heading for the big time.

Professional Leasing Consultant

Let me use this for an illustration and don't ever forget it as long as you live. You can't pay the professional doctor to come into his office and say to Mrs. Nash.

"I just finished your tests. You've got to have an operation, but before you decide here are the business cards of two doctors. I want you to go to their office. Tell them I sent you. I want you to let them run some tests. Then you decide which doctor you want to use."

Professional leasing consultant, you couldn't pay him to sell that way, but yet and still we go to his office. He has patients sitting all around the walls. Have you ever wondered why? The reason those patients are there is he's making decisions for his patients. As leasing consultants, we have to help our prospective residents make the correct decisions. We must help the potential resident make the decision. As a seller of anything in this world, we have to help that person sitting

191

across from us to make a decision that benefits both you and them. People want professionals to take charge and make decisions for them.

Do it the way I teach you, remembering, you are God's man or God's woman. Who would you send the customers to if you were God? To a person never mentioning God or to a person that's sold on God? That's all you've got to do. He tells us so clearly, *"If you do not confess me before men, I will not confess you before my Father, who is in heaven."*

Get smart and lease more apartment homes than you have ever experienced in your life. But you've got to believe these

Be Smart and Lease Apartment Homes

approaches and closes, practicing them over and over. In fact, everything I teach you, you've got to believe from the top of your head to the bottom of your feet. It will work when you apply the *"Wealth Building Scriptures and Tips"* daily. It's just as simple as that. Faith works. Put it to work for you.

Before they leave your office going out to inspect *their* apartment home and making that trip to see *their* new apartment home, always walk out in the yard with them. Point to the direction they need to go to this apartment home. Tell them you will be there waiting on them when they arrive back.

"Mr. and Mrs. Nash, get ready to move."

Those are the last words they've got to hear.

Practice these words. "Get ready to move." You don't think about what I'm saying here when you get ready to go out there to point out that apartment. It must come naturally. You've got to practice these words. That's why I have repeated this story in this book for you to follow it to the letter. I know it works; it worked for me. Plant in the minds of your prospective resident what to think about on the way to their new apartment home. "Get ready to move."

Do you know how long it's going to take them to inspect that apartment? They're out there getting ready to move. Now, walk out into the yard about the time you think they're coming back. When you see them coming, you're smiling and you're grinning. They're smiling and grinning.

Please don't ever forget this as long as you live, do not ask them what they think or do they like it, or do they want to look at more. Don't get jumpy; say:

"Come on back into my office. I'm going to get this one worked out for you."

If you mention that second apartment home or that third apartment home — no wonder you've got a lot of vacancies out there — because you are not doing it the way I teach you. You are only confusing your prospective residents by showing them so many beautiful apartment homes, giving too many choices and keeping them in the habit of "looking."

ဢ   ဢ

They're in front of your desk now in your office. This is the question.

"What name do you want to put the lease in?"

Notice, I haven't asked them do they want it, have I?

"What name do you want to put the lease in?"

If they give me that name, what are they telling me, *"AC, we want the apartment."* All I've got to do now is write up the lease. They don't have to tell me to write it up, I write it up and I turn it around so they can okay it.

I give the pen to the person that wants that lease in his or her name. Isn't that simple? Just that simple. Do it this way and you will not have to worry about any more vacancies tomorrow—period.

Now is the time to go to the Bible. What does it say? *"Ask and it shall be given you. Seek and ye shall find. Knock and it shall be opened unto you. For everyone that asketh, receiveth. He that seeketh, findeth. And to him that knocks, it shall be opened."*

Now you've got to have some people to call you tomorrow about leasing so you can make your sales goals. Or you've got to have people to call tomorrow so you can make your sales goals. Look in front of you, there is this sweet couple sitting in your office. You've got to look at it this way. They didn't hear anyone come in asking for you as a leasing consultant, did they? They didn't hear that. They didn't see anyone sitting out there in the reception room waiting for you, did they? Remember what I said in that egg story -- _crowds do create sales_. And if you are a leasing consultant, you are in the selling profession.

Now if they come to check out your apartment home community and they see people out there looking at your apartment homes or hear people come in asking for you, as the leasing consultant, you are in control. You and your apartment home community becomes a hot commodity in their perception.

Because of the added activity, your prospective residents become more interested in your community and become anxious concerning becoming a resident because they believe you may not have a lot of vacancies left. Additionally, they believe you are doing something right because of the other interested parties. They do not want to miss out on a good thing. Get smart and lease apartment homes.

Getting Management Approval

Let's talk about this business called getting them approved with your management. As a leasing consultant, you have a responsibility here to serve God's people. But you've got to let them know how to put in that foundation to get approved. You as the leasing consultant and

195

the prospective residents have got to team up together. You have got to make sure these people qualify. How are you going to do that? It says it so clearly in the Bible, *"When two or three gather in my name, I'm in the midst. Whatever you ask, I'll do it."*

You've got to believe this concept from the top of your head to the bottom of your feet. Helping these people is the way you get God's attention to work on your behalf. <u>Become more concerned about His people than you are about yourself.</u>

<u>You have a responsibility.</u> You can't just run a credit report and let the chips fall where they may. That's what's going to happen because you were not interested as a leasing consultant. Your job is to get these people approved by your management company.

Now, how can you do this? That's the question. *"When two or three gather in my name, I'm in the midst. Whatever you ask, I'll do."* Explain to your prospective resident, before you even order the credit report, you want the two of you to start saying the <u>23rd Psalms</u> together. Do this spiritual door opener from this day forward. You've got to believe this from the top of your head to the bottom of your feet. Repeating the 23rd Psalm is a powerful door opener!

.:PAUSE:. Wealth Building Scriptures
Week 10 – My Daily Commitment

1. Sunday – Play the role... Joseph story: <u>Genesis 39</u>.

2. Monday – "And the LORD said unto Moses, Write this *for* a memorial in a book, and rehearse *it* in the ears of Joshua: for I will utterly put out the remembrance of Amalek from under heaven." <u>Exodus 17:14</u>.

3. Tuesday - *"They that are delivered* from the noise of archers in the places of drawing water, there shall they rehearse the righteous acts of the LORD, *even* the righteous acts *toward the inhabitants* of his villages in Israel: then shall the people of the LORD go down to the gates." <u>Judges 5:11</u>.

4. Wednesday – "See that none render evil for evil unto any *man*; but ever follow that which is good, both among yourselves, and to all *men*." <u>1 Thessalonians 5:15</u>.

5. Thursday – "But the fruit of the Spirit is love, joy, peace, longsuffering, gentleness, goodness, faith, meekness, temperance: against such there is no law." <u>Galatians 5:22-23</u>.

6. Friday – "Two *are* better than one; because they have a good reward for their labour." Ecclesiastes 4:9;

7. Saturday – "Behold, I stand at the door, and knock: if any man hear my voice, and open the door, I will come in to him, and will sup with him, and he with me." <u>Revelation 3:20</u>.

8. Bonus – "Even so faith, if it hath not works, is dead, being alone." <u>James 2:17</u>; "But as many as received him, to them gave he power to become the sons of God, *even* to them that believe on his name:" <u>John 1:12</u>.

9. Bonus – "Ask, and it shall be given you; seek and ye shall find; knock, and it shall be opened unto you:" <u>Matthew 7:7</u>.

10. Bonus – "*Let your* conversation *be* without covetousness; and *be content* with such things as ye have: for he hath said, I will never leave thee, nor forsake thee." <u>Hebrews 13:5</u>; "And all things, whatsoever ye shall ask in prayer, believing, ye shall receive." <u>Matthew 21:22</u>.

11. Bonus – "The LORD *is* my shepherd; I shall not want. He maketh me to lie down in green pastures: he leadeth me beside the still waters. He restoreth my soul: he leadeth me in the paths of righteousness for his name's sake. Yea, though I walk through the valley of the shadow of death, I will fear no evil: for thou *art* with me; thy rod and thy staff they comfort me. Thou preparest a table before me in the presence of mine enemies: thou anointest my head with oil; my cup runneth over. Surely goodness and mercy shall follow me all the days of my life: and I will dwell in the house of the LORD forever." 23rd <u>Psalm</u>.

(Read Wealth Building Scriptures Aloud-3x Daily)

.:PAUSE:. Wealth Building Tips
Week 10 – My Daily Affirmation

1. Sunday – I will *act* to help my customers make the proper decisions.

2. Monday – I will practice getting referrals for two weeks in an effort to fit it into my personality.

3. Tuesday – I will practice perfecting my approaches and closes until they become a part of my personality.

4. Wednesday – My actions will be positive because I realize that for every action there is a reaction. I want positive reactions from others.

5. Thursday – I will persuade people by using the correct words in the correct tones.

6. Friday – I will help others make the correct decision.

7. Saturday – I am not ashamed of the Gospel of Jesus.

8. Bonus - I believe faith works and is working for me.

9. Bonus - Today I will ask Father God for what I need. I will look for it, knock on some doors and make some calls to get what He has promised me today.

10. Bonus - Today, I understand that Jesus never leaves me. He hears me when I speak to Him. I must believe that whatever I ask, He will do it—He will do it His way.

11. Bonus - When a bad situation appears, immediately I will say the 23rd Psalm with the situation in mind.

(Read Wealth Building Tips Aloud-3x Daily)

Chapter 11

Going One Step Further

Using the
P.A.U.S.E.®
(Practical Application and Use of the Scriptures Everyday)
Wealth Building System

"A Psalm of David. The LORD *is* my shepherd; I shall not want. He maketh me to lie down in green pastures: he leadeth me beside the still waters. He restoreth my soul: he leadeth me in the paths of righteousness for his name's sake. Yea, though I walk through the valley of the shadow of death, I will fear no evil: for thou *art* with me; thy rod and thy staff they comfort me. Thou preparest a table before me in the presence of mine enemies: thou anointest my head with oil; my cup runneth over. Surely goodness and mercy shall follow me all the days of my life: and I will dwell in the house of the LORD forever."

Psalm 23

Doing It God's Way®

Chapter **11**

Going One Step Further

23rd Psalm

N **ow, take it** a step further leasing consultants and readers of this book. <u>Get your Bible and take it to your office</u>. If that couple doesn't know the 23rd Psalms, show them where it is in your Bible. This is when you <u>pull out a copy of the 23rd Psalm for the couple</u>. Make copies of the 23rd Psalm if you have not; go to your local copy center and run off about 10-20 copies if you have to. Run copies for the next Mr. and Mrs. Nash and for yourself. You sit there and go over that 23rd Psalms with them. You learn it as if you don't know it and have the two of them learn it. Go over it with them in that office. Tell them to read it aloud 2 or 3 times a day, maybe 4 or 5 times a day. In fact, make this a way of life.

Start saying that 23rd Psalms all during the day. Why? Let me tell you why. This is an encouraging scripture. It will encourage you during the good days and the not so good days.

Explain to your prospective resident how to make this a way of life—using the scriptures like this example to overcome the obstacles and hurdles which life throws our way. Do not just make this a way of just getting an apartment home sale, but make this a way of life. You can share this experience with them—the "Traffic Stop" in the next section.

Tell them how you learned this. Now let me tell you what happened to me. People need to know how to do this, how to use the 23rd Psalm to bind the strongman in any situation. I don't care what the situation is, the principle is the same. God owns it all.

Traffic Stop

Traveling on Roswell Road one day, this police officer stopped me. He flashed his lights and I pulled over. You know when you have done something wrong. I don't know why he did it this way, but he parked 100 feet behind my car when I pulled over. By the time he put his feet on the paved street, heading towards me, I had asked God for forgiveness real quick. The police officer started walking towards my car.

I started saying <u>the 23rd Psalms, using "our" instead of "my"</u>, and I was watching him in the rearview mirror. It looked like he was in step with that 23rd Psalms. Just bouncing, coming towards me. He walked up to my car.

"Let me see your driver's license and insurance card."

If you could see my driver's license you would see me grinning. That requires practice. <u>Smiling and grinning creates sales.</u> You've got to be ready when you step up on that stand before the judge, before the audience on the stage of life. You've got to be grinning when you get up there and you have to be prepared. If not, you're going to end up with frowns on your face.

Smiles and grins create sales. <u>Smiles represents confidence and friendship.</u> Grins represent the jokes you tell to get them and keep them laughing; and purchasing your products and services. Get them happy and keep them happy.

Guess what this Caucasian police officer said to me? He had never seen me before; he was looking at my driver's license.

"Young man, why are you so excited?"

This is what he called me – "young man" -- I was 73 years young when this took place.

"You," he said, "are so excited this morning. What about a courtesy ticket?"

I didn't even know God had such a thing in the package—a courtesy ticket. I had never heard that word before that morning. This Caucasian brother didn't know me, had never seen me before in his life.

Notice now, how when you have a smile on your face, whenever you have a life situation like this one, you come out the winner. Take a hold of the situation with a smile. A smile will give the situation a new meter. Think success. Think victory. Twist a negative situation into a positive one with a smile. Do it because you will find that it works.

"I'm going to write it up as a courtesy warning," he said.

He gave me the courtesy ticket and went walking on back to his car. He had to walk about 100 feet back to his car. Why he parked that far behind me I do not know, but he did.

As we merged into traffic, 30 or 40 cars got between us. I had crossed Interstate 285 heading towards Decatur, Georgia. He passed by just waving. This Caucasian brother didn't know me from the next guy. Why was he waving at me going down Interstate 285 towards Decatur? In the Word, the 23rd Psalms starts like this, *"The Lord is my Shepherd, I shall not want."* This is a noteworthy experience, which I will never forget.

છ૭   ૦ક

Life Takes on
A New Meaning

Understand, these professional residents don't know this. As the professional leasing consultant, you are hearing this and making a decision as you read this. You've been put on notice on how to do this. Now you want to know if this is for real. But you, as the professional leasing consultant, have got to believe this concept from the top of your head to the bottom of your feet. You can't teach it nor use it unless you believe it. Let me put you on notice. Before this will work for you, you've got to do this program the way Christ did.

Jesus Christ didn't just read His Bible, hear the Word preached, tithe His money and give offerings. He got out there and got his hands filled with helping people. You have to have this type of attitude—to go out there and help your brothers and sisters. You've got to be this type of leasing consultant. Now you've got something. These people need to know this and you're in a very good position to teach them.

You want your rent, don't you? Teach them how to do this. Let them make this a way of life. The way you get God's attention to work on your behalf is become more concerned about His people than you are about yourself. Here is a tool to do just that—the 23rd Psalm.

These people want an apartment home. You have an apartment home for lease. God owns them. God owns you. And really, God owns those apartment homes also. If you take this attitude, you'll discover your management company will approve many of the applications you present to them. It's just as simple as that, and you have a job which you will keep because now you're "Doing it God's Way." This is the application of the faith principle.

If you do it the way I'm teaching, no man on earth can compete with you in the apartment home leasing business unless they are doing it God's way also. But wait a minute. Let us understand one another because <u>this is going to be a way of life now</u>.

<u>Bad credit, sickness and disease are going to be something of the past</u> when you read my books and listen to my CD's and use what I am teaching; and repeat the usage of the material. They are going to vanish from your world because <u>you're going to be thinking differently from now on</u>. If you think bad credit, that's what you've got. If you think you're sick, you're sick. If you think you've got disease, you've got disease. If you think your management will approve your potential apartment home tenant, approval percentages will go up. Keep listening.

Life's going to take on a new meaning when you <u>say aloud the Wealth Building Tips and Scriptures at the end of each</u>

chapter three times a day; one for each day of the week. One scripture and tip for every day of the week. That management company will love you as a leasing consultant because you know something they don't know. And your status as a leasing consultant will rise when you do it God's way. We are not in the business just to make a living, we're in the business to do it God's way. And your residents have got to know it that way.

They'll be able to stop paying traffic tickets because you have taught it to them. But you've got to believe these concepts from the top of your head to the bottom of your feet.

Perseverance is Key

Importunity
(Luke 11:5-13)

When you first start using this program, here comes two or three tests to see if you really will keep on doing it this way. First man turned you down. Second man turned you down also. Here comes that third man. He turns you down too. I challenge any man or woman to try the next one or the one that follows. See this is how you can see how many people don't believe God's Word. We get turned down two or three times and we think it won't work. We work by faith and not by sight. Keep at it!

Do not look at the circumstances, but stick to the script. Keep on doing it. Be hardheaded and keep on doing it. Life will take on a new meaning when you stick to the plan; persevere to the end, getting to the gold prize.

We go to court and we sit there and pay all of those fines. In the church every time the door is opened, we pay our tithes and our offerings; and you should be if you are not.

We go to court and you couldn't pay us to sit there and say that 23rd Psalm before that judge calls our name. I challenge you to start doing it that way. See what will happen. Believe the judge is going to throw it out and they will. _Say it. Know it. Believe it_. This is also a way to get your "borderline" people approved.

I know my methods work, but you've got to believe it. If you doubt it, you question it, or you want further clarification, remember, "the best proof is in the pudding." Do it, it works!

Inspecting
the Apartment

Let's talk about inspecting the apartment when the people move in. We're talking about running an apartment community. Do it the way I teach you. You won't ever have to worry about employment if you do it the way I teach you. You'll have people waiting in line to get an apartment in your community.

Inspect the apartment where your residents are to live three times:

1) When your residents first move in,

2) The first month after your residents have moved in, and

3) The second month after your residents have moved in.

This increases your credibility. When your residents move in, you as the leasing consultant, go out there to see if there's anything wrong. Carry a notepad and be concerned. If things are not right in there, get them fixed. If you have a maintenance man that can't fix it, get someone that can. That's the way you keep your residents.

Go through that apartment with the resident with a fine-toothed comb and do not short-change this visit. What do I mean when I say don't short-change it? Don't be in a hurry. Get serious with your job. Make sure your apartment home community is operating as the number one apartment home community in your area. You'll have more residents than you'll know what to do with. Make sure each apartment home is running in A+ condition; and one which you would not mind living in.

Get to know your residents by name. And when you go in that apartment and your residents have moved in, compliment them on the things that they have.

"Oh, that's a beautiful bedspread." "What a nice living set you have."

Oh, your residents will love you to death if you do this.

<u>Get their children's names</u> and call them by name. You see the little boy, pick him up and bounce him, but don't drop him. You're *"collecting rent"* when you get the prospective residents enamored with you. Now you're in the people business. When you realize you are in the people business—know that you are in the selling business.

Compliment Patsy on that beautiful sofa bed. This is the way you do it. It's so simple to operate this way. Little things like this helps you collect rent before its due.

This was the first day they moved in. We're talking about them paying the rent, now. Oh, they'll beat you paying your rent where you live, when you do the things I am sharing with you. This accommodating procedure will help your residents love you, trust you, believe in you and want to help you all the way—if you do things like this.

Next month, go back to that same apartment home on your rounds. (You do <u>have scheduled inspections throughout the year</u> don't you?) Sit the husband and the wife down and find out if there's anything else that needs to be done. And don't be jumpy. Some things you just cannot get done but make sure you give it your utmost to get everything done. At the very least, you must show interest in what their concerns are. This will show your resident that you genuinely care about them. <u>They will in turn tell someone about your attention to detail</u>. Those "someones" are your potential future residents.

You're talking about keeping your prospective and present residents. We're talking about keeping your residents, that's what we're talking about here and growing your apartment home community. You'll have more prospective residents than you'll know what to do with. I can't over-emphasize this.

We are not bringing in prospective residents just to collect rent. <u>We're sowing service in addition to bringing the prospective residents into our community</u>. We don't want to just collect their money and give them the least of what they are supposed to have or the least of what they expect.

We want to bring them in and give them the service they are supposed to have. You've got to do it this way. Remember, we are the servants of God and He sees everything we do. He can allow us to go up or He can allow us to go down. We are not getting by with anything. We are here to help the prospective residents.

The following month go back to that same new resident apartment. This time you'll do it the same way. Find out if there's anything wrong. *Don't forget to <u>compliment</u>. Don't forget to <u>congratulate</u> them* on how they bring their rent payment to the office on time.

Congratulate them on it. <u>Don't write them nasty letters</u> when they are behind. Write them good letters. <u>Get them thinking positively by sending them positive messages</u>. You will discover your job will be so simple. Congratulate them on paying on time. This is the way you do it.

Turn complaints into gold. Now if you get into a slump in your office and you do not have any new residents coming in, go out there and start inspecting the apartments of the residents you already have. Have a *"common courtesy"* inspection; one to *"fix any outstanding problems with their apartment home."*

Don't ask them for referrals. Just go out there and <u>be concerned about their complaints</u>. You will discover you will come out of that slump so fast and your residents will start paying on time. You may discover that your residents act more friendly towards one another through the kindness of your actions. <u>Actions are contagious</u>. Smile and be kind. <u>Let your actions be positive</u>.

You'll make more sales with this program than you'll know what to do with. This is the way you do it. This is apartment home leasing, the wealth building tips for you to follow to build your wealth. If you follow it, as a leasing consultant, you will love the newfound success you now have in your job.

℘   ℂ

.:PAUSE:. Wealth Building Scriptures
Week 11 – My Daily Commitment

1. Sunday – "My tongue shall speak of thy word: for all thy commandments *are* righteousness." Psalm 119:172.

2. Monday – Psalm 23.

3. Tuesday – "For the LORD shall be thy confidence, and shall keep thy foot from being taken." Proverb 3:26; "Cast not away therefore your confidence, which hath great recompence of reward." Hebrews 10:35.

4. Wednesday – "If a brother or sister be naked, and destitute of daily food, and one of you say unto them, Depart in peace, be *ye* warmed and filled; notwithstanding ye give them not those things which are needful to the body; what *doth it* profit?" James 2:16; Matthew 25:35-36; Matthew 25:31-46.

5. Thursday – "And we know that all things work together for good to them that love God, to them who are the called according to his purpose." Roman 8:28; James 1:2.

6. Friday – "I will delight myself in thy statues: I will not forget thy word." Psalm 119:16.

7. Saturday – "And if it seem evil unto you to serve the LORD, choose you this day whom ye will serve; whether the gods which your fathers served that were on the other side of the flood, or the gods of the Amorites, in whose land ye dwell: but as for me and my

house, we will serve the LORD." Joshua 24:15; Deuteronomy 10:12-13.

8. Bonus – "Ah, Lord GOD! Behold, thou hast made the heaven and the earth by thy great power and stretched out arm, and there is nothing too hard for thee:" Jeremiah 32:17; Luke 11:8.

9. Bonus – "I can do all things through Christ which strengthened me." Philippians 4:13; 2 Corinthians 5:7; Widow's Fast (1 Kings 17)

10. Bonus – "I rejoice therefore that I have confidence in you in all things." 2 Corinthians 7:16; Ephesians 3:12

11. Bonus – "If a brother or sister be naked, and destitute of daily food, and one of you say unto them, Depart in peace, be ye warmed and filled; notwithstanding ye give them not those things which are needful to the body; what doth it profit? James 2:15-16; Genesis 4:9.

12. Bonus – "Learn to do right! Seek justice, encourage the oppressed. Defend the cause of the fatherless, plead the case of the widow." Isaiah 1:17 (NIV)

13. Bonus – "And we know that all things work together for good to them that love God, to them who are the called according to his purpose." Roman 8:28; Mark 9:23; Matthew 19:26; Mark 10:27; Mark 14:36.

14. Bonus – "My brethren, count it all joy when ye fall into divers temptations;" James 1:2; Roman 8:28.

(Read Wealth Building Scriptures Aloud-3x Daily)

.:PAUSE:. Wealth Building Tips
Week 11 – My Daily Affirmation

1. Sunday – I will keep a Bible at the office and a copy of the 23rd Psalm to motivate and encourage people.

2. Monday – I will say the 23rd Psalm, using "our" instead of "my" which acts to resolve most situations.

3. Tuesday – I will smile more because it will increase my sales. I will smile with confidence as I speak.

4. Wednesday — I will get God's attention by finding a need and filling it.

5. Thursday – I am going to think differently and more positively from now on.

6. Friday — I will say aloud the *Wealth Building Tips and Scriptures* at the end of each chapter three times a day.

7. Saturday — I am not working just to make a living; I'm working to serve God in whatever I do.

8. Bonus –I will respond positively when two or three tests come to see if I really will keep on doing it this way.

9. Bonus – I will work by faith and not by sight. I will not look at the circumstances, but stick to the plan.

10. Bonus – I will *speak with confidence and belief.*

11. Bonus – I will know my neighbors by name.

12. Bonus – I will compliment and congratulate people on their successes; large or small.

13. Bonus – I will turn complaints into gold.

14. Bonus – My actions will be positive and contagious.

(Read Wealth Building Tips Aloud-3x Daily)

Chapter 12

Trigger Your Buyer's Imagination

Using the
P.A.U.S.E.®
(Practical Application and Use of the Scriptures Everyday)
Wealth Building System

We Must Put *Something* into Action
To Get the Expected Reaction We Desire.

Doing It God's Way®

Chapter 12

Trigger Your Buyer's Imagination

Sunday Brunch

Years ago I experienced this. My wife was looking through the newspaper and she saw an advertisement. *"Sunday Brunch."* She came to me and said.

"We have got to go there and eat this Sunday afternoon. They have a Sunday brunch for dinner."

The first thing we thought about was a buffet. So we headed to the restaurant, expecting a spread of food. Many other older people saw the advertisement in the newspaper too, because they were there at the restaurant when we arrived. Our imaginations had been triggered by the words, *"Sunday Brunch"* in the newspaper and so were theirs.

We went into the restaurant but we didn't see the food spread that we were expecting. We were thinking there would be a spread of food on the tables. All we would have had to do was go around and select our entrees. This would have been a *"Sunday Brunch."*

Words Trigger Our Imaginations

When the hostess came and got us and carried us to the table, I noticed on the menu in large letters *"Sunday Brunch."* There was no large spread of food. And there was no *"Sunday Brunch,"* but we didn't leave. We really enjoyed that *"Sunday Brunch."*

My wife asked a waitress. "I thought the newspaper said Sunday Brunch? Is this it?" she asked.

The waitress replied, "This *is* the Sunday Brunch."

That food was so good and delicious. When *triggering imaginations, we have to have something which people find worthy of their time, money, and effort.* You have to have something to back up what you are promoting.

If that ad had not read the way it did, we would not have been there that Sunday afternoon. And most likely, that crowd that we saw there would not have been there either. Crowds create interest. Because there was a crowd of people waiting, my wife and I stayed interested in the *"Sunday Brunch."* Crowds do create sales. If that ad had not been worded that way, *"Sunday Brunch,"* we would not have been there. We would have missed a good thing. That *"Sunday Brunch."*

Right Man for the Job
(Psalm 121)

My **partner,** M.J. Reese, who is my brother-in-law and I bought the Cascade Cabana Apartments on Cascade Road in Atlanta, Georgia. After we bought those apartments, we discovered there was not much cash flow. We only had enough cash flow to hire one man.

This one man had to do everything. Keep the yards clean, do the maintenance, collect the rent; in other words, he did everything. But before this one man came, we had about forty-five vacant apartment homes. This was back when they were giving apartments away, in the 1970's. This is when Jimmy "Who?" was running for President. Everyone remembers President Jimmy Carter. We had a real tax shelter, but no money because we had forty-five vacancies. I was not in the tax shelter business, but in the "making money" business.

I put an ad in the Atlanta-Journal Constitution for an apartment manager. I had asked God to give me someone who could do everything which we needed to get done. When Bobby Little came into my office for an interview, he was trembling. He was shaking. He was a recovering alcoholic.

God said, "Put him on the job."

This was the best business decision that I have ever made in my life.

Bobby Little was filled with "can'ts."

"Mr. Brown," Bobby said, "I can't paint. I can't collect money. I can't mow the lawn."

I just listened to his, *"I can't do this. And I can't do that."* Remember, God told me to hire this man who was filled with *"can'ts."*

This appears not to be the correct thing to do: hire Bobby Little, a recovering alcoholic, that's sitting there trembling. Now what did I do? I pulled out my Bible and taught Bobby how to do the Pathway to Success®. I instructed him to do it every morning just like Jesus Christ did when God placed Him on this earth.

Now, what did Jesus Christ do when He walked this earth? He got up <u>early each morning</u>, <u>looked to Heaven and prayed</u> to the Father. This is why God sent Him here to set the example for you and I to follow, because <u>each one of us is born in God's image</u> and <u>if Jesus Christ did it then you and I can do it too</u>. So I immediately followed Father God's direction.

This one man that I hired was a recovering alcoholic. In fact when I hired him he was shaking. He was nervous and had never managed apartments before. But God told me to hire this one man. Remember his name: Bobby Little. When you get your *"Bobby Little"* sitting across the desk from you, remember what you are learning here. Do not forget this.

Before we hired him prospective buyers wanted to buy the

apartments. They gave us a contract of $700,000. We would not sell for $700,000– no way —that was too cheap. I put Bobby Little on the job to work on those apartment homes.

Bobby Little would beg me every Friday, "Mr. Brown put me an ad in the paper."

I would write that ad up just like Bobby described it.

"Tell the people to come to the beautiful Cascade Cabana Apartments to come and blow their horns. Blow their horns three times." One for the Father, One for the Son, one for the Holy Spirit and one for Bobby Little because he was also doing the maintenance and the horn would signal him to stop and come give them assistance.

I would listen to Bobby talking to the prospective residents.

"Come and see our beautiful apartments with their beautiful hardwood floors, remember to blow your horn three times."

Bobby would stop working and go out to meet his prospective residents. In six months Bobby had a waiting list of prospective residents.

This is the way I worded my ad; we are talking about triggering the prospective resident's imagination.

"There are two-bedroom apartments and one-bedroom apartments." That is what I said in the ad.

In the Atlanta Constitution Newspaper the ad continued:

"Beautiful hardwood floors, apartments renting for ONLY $350 PER MONTH. Move in today."

When I designed that ad in the newspaper, I made these words large in caps: *"ONLY $350 PER MONTH,"* and that stood out from the other parts of the ad.

I believe in trying things. This ad idea was new to me. At the completion of the ad, I was saying something like this.

"Come out and see them for yourself."

And I gave the location.

"Just circle around and stop. And blow your horn three times. The manager will be glad to let you see the apartments."

The reason I wanted them to blow the horn three times is because the manager was the only worker there. He was doing everything. Bobby Little would stop his work and lease the apartment home. In six months we had a house full of people.

Two German gentlemen, Mr. Winkles and his son from Canada came out to look at the apartments to purchase them. Remember, I had a $700,000

Our Job is to Solve Problems. The Key is Faith

---

contract in hand from another group of prospective buyers.

Mr. Winkles and his son bought that property for a sales price of one million dollars, because we knew how to trigger the prospective buyer's imagination. So impressive was Bobby Little to Mr. Winkles that Mr. Winkles would not close the transaction unless Bobby Little came with the package. Mr. Winkles' imagination was triggered by him seeing that Bobby Little was doing everything at the apartment home community and what potential he had for Mr. Winkle's new investment.

What was so exciting about this man Bobby Little is he was a one-man show, managing eighty-five apartments. Guess what? Bobby Little went with the package. I was getting Bobby ready for another project and did not want him to go. But I also wanted to close the deal on those apartment homes. I realized that if God sent me one "Bobby Little" he could send me another. <u>Do not hold on too tightly to what you have</u>. God may have another use for it; and it may be for someone else. This gives God an opportunity to move on your behalf; remember, the key is faith.

<u>Our job is to solve problems</u>. We have a tendency to run from problems; our own problems and the problems of other people. <u>Our job is to solve problems</u>. God helps us solve them as long as we bring Him along. That is the way you make your fortune. <u>Take a problem and turn it into millions</u>.

The Bible says, "<u>press the battle to the gate</u>," which is what it is talking about; <u>attack a problem head-on</u>. This separates the boys from the men and the girls from the women. We must all understand that <u>all things are possible to those who believe</u>. Remember, God works through faith, not eyesight.

Let me say this before we leave this. Why did I hire Bobby Little? This is the way I do business. I opened my mouth and I asked God who I should hire after I placed an ad in the newspaper.

My experiences have been this way for 48 years. When God sends a man or a woman, if you are doing what Christ did

227

when He walked this earth, <u>God is going to send you the best in the business</u>. It is just as simple as this. Bobby Little had never managed apartments before. That is the way I do my hiring—follow the Holy Spirit's advice.

<u>I follow God every step of the way</u>. And if you change it around when God gives you instruction, by adding your two cents in it, it will not work for you. Why? Because God is a good God and a very jealous God. I always get the best in the business. If I can do it this way you can too. This is a very important step in a businessperson's career.

Place your ad in the newspaper. <u>After you do that, open your mouth to God and ask Him to send you the best in the business, describing the position to God</u>. If you question it or want further clarification, there is none. When Bobby Little accepted what I was teaching him and fitted it into his personality, he could talk about those beautiful hardwood floors just like he was eating a piece of cake. Just think, a recovering alcoholic, why could he do it? Because God put Bobby Little on the job, he could do everything and then some.

For forty-eight years I used this procedure which I got from the Holy Spirit. I stay in that direction, in that decision, in that goal until God gives me another direction, decision, or goal to follow. Know <u>if God does not give me another direction, I will open my mouth and ask for it</u>. <u>God is obligated to give me an answer</u>.

Now when God gives you and answer and if a man comes along and criticizes your decision, do not change it. God knew

228

just what he wanted you to do. Do not listen to the criticism. Follow God. God is a loving God and He is a jealous God.

Apartments
According to Income

Let me say it for what it is worth. We have got to be doing what Jesus Christ did when He walked this earth. Not just reading our Bibles, hearing the Word preached, tithing our money and giving offerings—no, we have got to go further than that. <u>We have to help others solve their problems and practice turning tears into joy</u>. It is so simple to operate this way. It only takes desire and practice.

Let me take you a step further. I owned Glenwood Village Apartments, one hundred and fifty units. I had trouble getting people to move in during the first year. No one would call me. Trying to get people to move into those apartment homes was a real pain.

I placed an ad in the newspaper. This is the way I worded my ad. *"We rent these apartments according to INCOME"*. And that stood out in my ad in caps: *"WE RENT THESE APARTMENTS ACCORDING TO **INCOME**"*.

Some of you may believe that this maneuver is not "above board" because the reader may think the ad is talking about their income instead of the apartment home leasing costs.

229

That is not true because the advertisement was talking about one-bedroom apartment homes renting or leasing for less than two-bedroom apartment homes. It is true, one-bedroom apartment homes do lease or rent for more than two-bedroom apartment homes. If you don't believe that is true, look at your application. And if you do not have the income for two-bedroom apartment homes, you may have the income for a one-bedroom apartment home—"according to income."

When you bring a prospective resident in, the first or the second question you ask is: *What is your income?* The prospective resident can't deny that you are going to ask that question. The prospective resident expects you to ask that question.

When I put that ad together I didn't have any more trouble renting apartments. It is true, the residents that called were thinking they were going to get a deal. We have got to understand it this way – we have got to try things—new things, because we all love to eat.

In other words, be a doer of the Word. This is the spirit of Joseph in operation. This is allowing the examples of Joseph to play out in your daily experience. I wasn't cheating anyone, I just knew how to manipulate the circumstance for both our benefits. The prospective residents benefited by moving into highly-serviced quality apartment homes which they would not have seen otherwise. I benefited from their residency.

If we just sit there and do it the same old way without success and don't try new things, we have the potential to go down the tubes. And it is our own faults if we do not try to do things differently.

It is often said that insanity is doing things the same way and expecting a different result than what you have been getting. <u>Do things differently to get different results</u>; <u>the results that you need and want</u>. We have got to have traffic to lease apartment homes. If we don't try things, we will always wonder where the traffic is.

<u>Faith without works is death</u>. If you want to get rid of your vacancies, listen. If you are leasing apartment homes you have got to go by a script—a sales presentation. You want two presentations; one presentation for the telephone and one for prospective residents in your office. You have got to have the words and you have got to have them right. You can't just sit there and ad lib and say anything—oh, no. You will be surprised at what you can do with a script in front of you.

<u>I always prepare a script</u> to go by no matter which field I am in. I ask the Lord to give me the right words. Then I practice the presentation until I get it just right, practicing on employees, family members, or friends.

Take a script and adapt it to your situation. Use it and revolutionize your apartment home leasing business or whatever kind of business you are in.

Stop Doing It on Your Own

I **highly recommend** that you <u>do the *Pathway to Success*® every morning</u>, seven days a week; along with your "Daily Wealth Building Affirmations and Commitments." <u>As a business owner or manager</u>, do it as I teach it in my Wealth Building books, cassettes and CD's. We have got to understand that God makes a way where there was none. We can't do it alone. The Holy Spirit has been my teacher for a period of 48 years and the Holy Spirit wants to be your teacher. Stop attempting to do it on your own.

Do the *Pathway to Success*® every morning and between every reading, lift those hands and praise God thanking Him for that opportunity. We are talking about triggering the buyer's imagination and getting him or her to call for an appointment; or purchase your product or service, *"Doing it God's Way."*

Let me take you to the Real Estate business. I sold Real Estate for twenty plus years; selling single-family homes. I wanted others to go into the Real Estate business. I tried my level best to talk people into going into the Real Estate business. I even had seminars.

232

People would come and hear the sales people stand up and talk about all the money they were making. Nevertheless, the people would not come into the Real Estate business. I wanted them to go full-time. That is the only way you are going to make any money. You have got to go full-time. Moreover, I tried and I tried and I tried. They would not give up those full-time jobs.

Earn as You Learn

I was in my *Pathway to Success*® class one morning. I heard these words: *"Earn as you Learn."* You can't do without that *Pathway to Success*® every morning because God knows what each individual needs. If you are trying to do this stuff on your own, if you are seeking success on your own, it will not work. You can get in a bind and lose everything you got. You got to look at it this way, if it were not for God, you and I would not even be here. In

Read Your Word
Do Your
Church Work
and Do the Word

my *Pathway to Success*® class, the only ones there was God, his Son Jesus, the Holy Spirit and AC Brown. I heard these words: *"Earn as you Learn."* I used these words to get people into the Real Estate business.

From then on, I had a full house every night at that Real Estate seminar. People were begging me to go full-time. They

233

would call every two or three minutes to come to that seminar. Once I had five people to pass the Real Estate examination in one crack. Just those few words I heard, made all the difference: *"Earn as you Learn."* We are talking about triggering the buyer's imagination.

I had more Real Estate sales people full-time than I knew what to do with. If I can do it this way, you can too. That took care of that problem. But I had to stay in that *Pathway to Success*® class every morning around three am in the morning to understand how to do it.

Jesus Christ did not just sit and read His Bible (the Pentateuch), hear the Scripture preached, tithe His money and give offerings. Jesus Christ got up every morning and talked to the Father. What about you and I? We are born in the image of God. If we don't do it this way, we are going to always wonder where it is. If it were not for God, you and I wouldn't even be here. <u>We are born in His image</u> and the way we get God's attention to work on our behalf is to become more concerned about God's people than we are about ourselves.

As a professional, I don't care if you are selling Real Estate, leasing apartment homes, selling automobiles or whatever. It is your job as a professional to teach these buyers and residents what to do and how to do it. You want to sell them an automobile, you want to sell them a home, and you want to lease them an apartment home, don't you? Why not teach them, while you work with them.

234

When you read my books, listen to my cassettes and CD's you are going to discover bad credit, sickness, and disease are going to be something of the past. When you start thinking the way I teach you, your life will not be the same. When you start practicing my Wealth Building System your life will change for the best.

Rent to Buy

Talk their benefits. If you are in the automobile business, the Real Estate business, the apartment home leasing business, whoever you are or whatever kind of business you are in, do it the way I teach it. You will revolutionize that business if you do it the way I teach it. It is no guesswork. It is the procedure that you are using that is working or not working for you.

Let me take this a step further. We are talking about triggering the prospective customer's imagination and get them calling. Let me take you a step further.

When We Talk
Their Benefits
We Sell People
What They Want

As an investor, if you own that property you can use "RENT TO BUY", but you got to know how to use it. You have got to be willing to go either way the buyer wants to go. This means they are coming to "Rent to Buy."

235

Example: You prepare two packages, one for rent and one to buy. You have to do your homework. When they come back to close the transaction, you present them with what the monthly payments and the taxes will be on the home, the documentation from the mortgage company and the appreciation schedule from an accounting firm.

As a professional, present them to your clients and compare what the rental versus the mortgage payments on the home will be and when they compare the two, under your direction, with the documentation, they will want to purchase the home instead of renting the home. It is easy to sell when you do the research.

As an investor, carry them the way you want them to go. You will discover that if you <u>have the correct words </u>and you <u>use them correctly</u>, you can take the buyer either way you want them to go. But you have got to be talking their benefits. It is just as simple as that. If they qualify to buy, then make your presentation so attractive, that they will want to buy. The more you practice your presentation, the more buyers will buy.

You have got to know how to sell, if not, I would recommend you not use this technique. The words have to be right and you cannot ad lib. Put your script together and practice it but keep in mind, the buyer who is listening to the words that comes out of your mouth. <u>If you got the words and you got them right you will be amazed at what you can do with this procedure.</u> Rent to buy requires practice, drill and rehearsal.

.:PAUSE:. Wealth Building Scriptures
Week 12 – My Daily Commitment

1. Sunday – "I say unto you, Though he will not rise and give him, because he is his friend, yet because of his importunity he will rise and give him as many as he needeth." Luke 11:8.

2. Monday – "But when the multitudes saw it, they marvelled; and glorified God, which had given such power unto men." Matthew 9:8.

3. Tuesday – Bonus – "For I was an hungred, and ye gave me meat: I was thirsty, and ye gave me drink: I was a stranger, and ye took me in: naked and ye clothed me: I was sick, and ye visited me: I was in prison, and ye came unto me." Matthew 25:35-36; Matthew 25:31-46.

4. Wednesday – "Ask, and it shall be given you; seek, and ye shall find; knock, and it shall be opened unto you:" Matthew 7:7; Luke 11:9.

5. Thursday – "So God created man in his own image, in the image of God created he him; male and female created he them." Genesis 1:27; Colossians 3:9-10.

6. Friday – A good man leaves an inheritance for his children's children, but a sinner's wealth is stored up for the righteous." Proverb 13:22.

7. Saturday – "Jesus looked at them and said, "With man this is impossible, but with God all things are possible." Matthew 19:26.

8. Bonus – "And if it seem evil unto you to serve the LORD, choose you this day whom ye will serve; whether the gods which your fathers served that were on the other side of the flood, or the gods of the Amorites, in whose land ye dwell: but as for me and my house, we will serve the LORD." <u>Joshua 24:15</u>.

9. Bonus – "And we know that all things work together for good to them that love God, to them who are the called according to his purpose." <u>Romans 8:28</u>.

10. Bonus – "Even so faith, if it hath not works, is dead, being alone." <u>James 2:17</u>.

(Read Wealth Building Scriptures Aloud-3x Daily)

.:PAUSE:. Wealth Building Tips
Week 12 – My Daily Affirmation

1. Sunday – I will trigger the imaginations of people by offering people things worthy of their time and money.

2. Monday – I will create interest by creating crowds.

3. Tuesday – I will look to Heaven, praying to the Father, knowing that I am in the "help one another" business.

4. Wednesday – I believe God is going to send me the best in the business. I will open my mouth, asking God to send me the best in the business.

5. Thursday – I am born in God's image and if Jesus Christ did it then I can do it too.

6. Friday– I will not give away what I own to evil ideas and purposes.

7. Saturday – I will be successful because all things are possible to those who believe. I believe.

8. Bonus – I follow Father God every step of the way.

9. Bonus – I will manipulate circumstances for the benefits of all involved.

10. Bonus – I will apply faith to my work by preparing and practicing my presentations.

(Read Wealth Building Tips Aloud-3x Daily)

Chapter 13

How to Succeed in Any Field

Using the
P.A.U.S.E. ®
(Practical Application and Use of the Scriptures Everyday)
Wealth Building System

"The voice of rejoicing and salvation is in the tabernacles of the righteous: the right hand of the LORD doeth valiantly."

Psalm 118:15

Doing It God's Way®

Chapter 13

How to Succeed
in Any Field

Acknowledge
to God First

(Proverbs 3:5-6)

Let me start this off this way. I go on no job, I open up no business, I join no church unless I open my mouth and acknowledge to God and let God direct my path. Whatever answer comes back, I follow it to the letter. I don't know about you, but I want to be in a church home that is tailor-made for me.

All churches are not tailor-made for AC Brown. I'm trying to go somewhere; and so should you. My experiences have been this way for forty-eight years.

If we are not in that church home that is tailor-made for us, we are always going to wonder where it is. That is the way I do it and I don't care what field I go into.

A man with a C and D transcript from college; I'm going to run rings around you, if you don't do it the way I do it. Through God all things are possible to

him that believeth. <u>I'm going to do that **Pathway to Success**® every morning, seven days a week.</u> Didn't Jesus Christ get up every morning and talk to the Father, what about you and I?

Along with my church work I'm going to go out there and <u>practice changing tears into joy.</u> If I can do it this way you can too. We are talking about how to succeed in any field regardless of your educational background. If I know how to do something and I see Tom has a problem with it, if I do not take time out of my busy schedule and help Tom and teach Tom how to do this, I am going nowhere with God and you are not either.

Be a Doer of the Word

I **was traveling** in the elevator at Emory University Hospital when a disturbing situation came into perspective. When you see a disturbing situation, God expects you to move in. That is Jesus' program. Not just reading your Bible, hearing the Word preached, tithing your money, and giving offerings; you have got to do these two things together—field work and church work. I have said this once and I am going to say it again as a reminder. You have got to look at it this way.

Jesus says, *"he who believes in me, the works that I do shall he do also even greater works than these shall he do because I go into my Father. Whatever he shall ask in my son's name that will I do that the Father may be glorified in the son."*

Who is Jesus talking to? Doesn't it sound like Jesus is talking to you and me? That church is in us. When we go out there and we do not put forth any effort to use that church in us, it is just like that church doesn't even exist.

God Keeps His Eyes and Ears Fixed on Us

I was traveling on that elevator at Emory University Hospital with approximately 13 other people. There was a lady crying on this elevator. The people that were standing around this lady were asking her if she was all right.

"Are you all right?" They asked the lady.

Jesus didn't do it that way. No. He moves in. I couldn't stand there and ask this lady, *"Are you all right?"* I had to find out what was wrong and I didn't mind these people standing there looking at the show. No, not at all. I'm only trying to please one God and one Jesus.

All this other stuff you could dump in the Atlantic Ocean because if you don't understand God and his Son Jesus you have nothing. I walked over to the lady and I asked her what was wrong. I knew God had that eye on me. He keeps that eye on me and He keeps an eye on you too. He never takes it off. This is what that lady said to me.

"My baby is upstairs real sick and the doctors do not know what to do for my baby."

"Get off at the next floor," I said to this lady. "I know what to do for your baby."

I still carry these prayers with me everywhere I go and I pass these prayers out and I teach people how to use this prayer. If they don't do it, I'm off the hook because I went the way Christ went. He met people that did not do what He said do. You are going to meet people that are not going to do what you say do. But once you take that move and do it, you have fulfilled your duty.

We got off at the next floor. I taught this lady how to use this prayer. I'm also teaching you in my books, cassettes, and CD's how to use this prayer. I taught this lady to pray the Blood of Jesus prayer every day on five people who have some type of problem. Then I taught her how to pray this prayer on herself everyday, three times a day. Then I asked her to pray the Blood of Jesus prayer on her baby three times a day, only the first name and the last name. Notice I put the baby last. Why? *"Seek ye first the kingdom of God and all these things will be added unto you."* What things? I told you that I averaged selling 10 to 15 homes per month, every month, working six days a week.

I have been into several fields and made millions in each field. That is those *things* that God is talking about. But you got to do it all together. And it is so simple to do it this way. I'm talking about making this procedure a lifestyle. This will allow you to succeed in any field regardless of your educational background.

I asked for that baby's name and God heard that. I said to this lady when I was leaving for her to call me when the baby made a turn-around. I had to wrap that baby with the Blood of Jesus three times a day. I did it until this lady called me. She called me six months later. One morning I was getting ready to go to church.

"Mr. Brown, she said, "the baby made a turn around and the doctors did not know what happened."

That is the way you succeed in any field regardless of your educational background. If I can do it this way, you can to.

When that lady called me that Sunday morning she wanted to give me five more names of people who she thought needed prayer. When you read your Bible it says, *"the laborers are few and the harvest is plentiful."* I challenge any man or woman to go in that direction. No person on earth can compete with you if you do it the way I teach you.

Standing at the
Gate Crying

Let me take you another step further. We are talking about how to succeed in any field regardless of your educational background. My son was facing 15 years. He was in the jail in Athens, Georgia. The day before the trial, my wife and I decided to go and visit him. As we entered the gate at the Athens jail, I spotted this lady that was approximately 80 years of age standing at the gate crying.

We are talking about seeking ye first in the kingdom of God and all these things will be added unto you. What things? My son was facing 15 years. I don't care what goes on in my life or in my household I don't get in a pity-party.

I didn't get in a pity-party because my son was facing 15 years. But I knew in order to get him out of it, I had to press the battles to the gate. That is why I couldn't pass that lady. I couldn't keep on walking to see my son and not stop to find out why she was crying.

God's eye stays on us. Awe, c'mon you know we can't fool God. I walked over to this lady and I asked her what was wrong. She said my husband is in jail. He got beat up last night. I gave the cab driver my last eight dollars to come out here to see him. They will not let me go in because I do not have the proper ID.

"Come on," I said to this lady, "let's go back to the jail and go in."

She asked this question. "How are you going to do that? I just left there. I gave the cab driver my last $8 and they would not let me go in because I do not have the proper ID."

"Come on let's go back to the same jail," I said to this lady, "and go in."

"I just left there," she said. "How are you going to do that?"

I said as we walked, "We are going to say the <u>23rd Psalm</u> together because He tells us so clearly when two or three gather in my name, I'm in the midst. Whatever you ask I will do it.' "

This is the twenty-third Psalm using "our" instead of "my" creating a plural, inclusive prayer.

Take What You Read in the Bible and Turn it into Action

"The Lord *is* our shepherd, we shall not want. He maketh us to lie down in green pastures: he leadeth us beside the still waters.

He restoreth our souls: he leadeth us in the paths of righteousness for his name's sake. Yea, though we walk through the valley of the shadow of death, we will fear no evil: for thou *art* with us; thy rod and thy staff, they comfort us.

Thou preparest a table before us in the presence of our enemies: thou anointest our heads with oil; our cups runneth over.

Surely goodness and mercy shall follow us all the days of our lives: and we will dwell in the house of the LORD for ever." Psalm 23

Yes we got in. When we walked up, before the jailer could get those real ugly words out of his mouth, out walks the head jailer.

"Lady, I'm going to let you go in this time. Do not come back in here anymore without the proper ID."

We are not talking about going in the next time are we? We are talking about going in right now. When we entered the jail the lady looked back at me and asked me this question.

"What church do you go to?"

This has been my experience for 48 years. Church people must learn how to take to the hurting world, what they read and hear from the Bible. We must prove to the hurting brothers and sisters that we have a solution for them. They will then beat a path to the church doors.

℘   ℭ

Go to the Hospital
and Pray

Early the next morning, I heard that voice. My son's trial was that afternoon. Early that next morning do you know what God said to me?

"I want you to go to Grady Hospital (in Atlanta) this morning and pray on 150 people. Go from room to room."

I had never done this before. But when God gives me a message like that, "*Go to the hospital and pray*," I'm on my way. I'm going. That was nothing but a test to see if I would do it. You got to understand my son's trial was that afternoon in Athens.

He wanted to give me an examination to see if I was brave enough to do it. This is what God wants you to do. Go out there. Along with your church work, go out there. Why learn all of that scripture and do all

Go into the World
Act Out the Bible

that church work if you are not going to use it for God out in the field? Do not sit there and wonder who it is or where it is; or who for or what for. Go out there and check it out. Do not sit there and wonder where it is. Go out there. Sure, I have been out there many times and nothing happens.

All I did was stand in my tracks and lift my hands as tall as I could and praised God. Thanking Him for that opportunity of going out there and checking it out. We got to look at it this way, God owns it all and without Him, you and I cannot do anything. That is the way we succeed in any field regardless of our educational background. You got to believe it from the top of your head to the bottom of your feet.

When I arrived at the 150th patient's room, the boys in blue, the police, came in from downtown Atlanta with handcuffs and put them on me. They proceeded to carry me downtown. The fine was $60. God told me to carry $60 with me. God knows what is going to happen before it happens. My son's trial was that afternoon.

In Front of the Judge

Enroute to Athens, Georgia here comes another test. If we waiver just one second of an inch we are going to miss that blessing. I said the 23rd Psalms on the way to Athens. I did not talk to my wife. I could not afford to talk to her and get into a pity-party, because she was surely in one. If you get into a pity party, you are going to miss the blessing. I did not even play the car radio.

While sitting in the Athens courtroom waiting for my son to stand up in front of that judge, I had my feet flat on the floor saying the 23rd Psalm. And I believed from the top of my head to the bottom of my feet.

When my son stood up in front of that judge, that judge looked at him eyeball to eyeball. Then he turned real quickly and looked out the window into space for approximately five minutes. Then he turned and looked back at my son after he had looked at the file real quickly.

"Son," he said to my son, "go home."

I don't know how you interpret this experience I had with my son. I was acting as a vessel for God attempting to save my son, save my son 15 years of his life. But you have got to understand before I could do this I had to seek ye first the kingdom of God. You got to understand that lady that was crying at the gate when we went into that jail is one of God's children. And those people at Grady Hospital are also God's children.

"Seek ye first the kingdom of God and all these things will be added unto you." That is the way I've done it for 48 years. No person on earth can compete with you if you do it the way I teach you. That's the way and the only way we are going to build our wealth.

.:PAUSE:. Wealth Building Scriptures
Week 13 – My Daily Commitment

1. Sunday – "Trust in the LORD with all thine heart; and lean not unto thine own understanding. In all thy ways acknowledge him, and he shall direct thy paths." Proverbs 3:5-6.

2. Monday – "Blessed is the man that walketh not in the counsel of the ungodly, nor standeth in the way of sinners, nor sitteth in the seat of the scornful. But his delight is in the law of the LORD; and in his law doth he meditate day and night." Psalm 1:1-2; "Let the proud be ashamed; for they dealt perversely with me without a cause: but I will meditate in thy precepts." Psalm 119:78.

3. Tuesday – "Verily, verily, I say unto you, He that believeth on me, the works that I do shall he do also; and greater works than these shall he do; because I go unto my Father." John 14:12.

4. Wednesday – "Behold, the eye of the LORD is upon them that fear him, upon them that hope in his mercy;" Psalm 33:18; "The eyes of the LORD are upon the righteous, and his ears are open unto their cry." Psalm 34:15.

5. Thursday – "The LORD is my shepherd; I shall not want. He maketh me to lie down in green pastures: he leadeth me beside the still waters. He restoreth my soul: he leadeth me in the paths of righteousness for his

name's sake. Yea, though I walk through the valley of the shadow of death, I will fear no evil: for thou art with me; thy rod and thy staff they comfort me. Thou preparest a table before me in the presence of mine enemies: thou anointest my head with oil; my cup runneth over. Surely goodness and mercy shall follow me all the days of my life: and I will dwell in the house of the LORD for ever." Psalm 23.

6. Friday – "Confess your faults one to another, and pray one for another, that ye may be healed. The effectual fervent prayer of a righteous man availeth much." James 5:16.

7. Saturday – "Go ye therefore, and teach all nations, baptizing them in the name of the Father, and of the Son, and of the Holy Ghost: Teaching them to observe all things whatsoever I have commanded you: and, lo, I am with you always, even unto the end of the world. Amen." Matthew 28:18-19.

8. Bonus – "But seek ye first the kingdom of God, and his righteousness; and all these things shall be added unto you." Matthew 6:33.

(Read Wealth Building Scriptures Aloud-3x Daily)

.:PAUSE:. Wealth Building Tips
Week 13 – My Daily Affirmation

1. Sunday – I will trust Father God in all my decisions, which He approves.

2. Monday – I will do the *Pathway to Success*® every morning, seven days a week.

3. Tuesday – I will live my life as though the power of Jesus Christ resides in me.

4. Wednesday – I know God is watching me, therefore I will live a righteous life.

5. Thursday – I know success is mine even when it looks like I am defeated. God will ensure that I am always victorious in all that I do.

6. Friday – I will take the time out of my busy schedule to go help someone who is less fortunate than I am. I will pray for someone to help turn his or her tears into joy.

7. Saturday – During this week, I will go into the world and act out the actions of Christ Jesus.

8. Bonus – I will seek God first with the understanding that because I honor Him, He will magnify my work so I may achieve my goals.

(Read Wealth Building Tips Aloud-3x Daily)

Chapter 14

How to Run Thieves Away

Using the
P.A.U.S.E. ®
(Practical Application and Use of the Scriptures Everyday)
Wealth Building System

"Let the proud be ashamed; for they dealt perversely with me without a cause: *but* I will meditate in thy precepts."

Psalm 119:78

Doing It God's Way®

Chapter 14

How to Run
Thieves Away

A Lot of Wisdom

Over the years, I have discovered many ways of preventing loss in my businesses. My brother-in-law and sisters-in-law have taught me so much over the years. Relatives do have a lot of wisdom. One idea my brother-in-law, Marshall Reese taught me was when someone asked for a favor or a loan from my Real Estate company, ask them to put it in writing and sign a commitment.

Marshall Reese had experienced a Real Estate salesperson asking for a loan against a commission on a house which he was about to sell. Marshall Reese asked the salesperson to put it in writing, offering him his pad to write it on.

The salesperson never did return with that pad because he did not have any sale going. Marshall Reese probably saved his company thousands of dollars with this one technique.

I was once told by the Georgia Water Department that the water supplying one of my apartment buildings was about to be cut off because of excessive use. I asked them to install a new meter because I did not see where that much water was being used. They did so, but the new meter did not make a difference. They insisted that I owed $40,000 for the water. I had begun the process to refinance the apartments and the Water Department placed a lien against the property.

Another lesson I learned over the years is that people are more willing to negotiate money with women than with men. Using my experience, and that knowledge, I sent my wife Lea to the Water Department with $10,000 cash and instructions to try and settle the account. Sure enough, Lea was able to walk out with the account settled for $10,000.

80   03

Choosing a CPA

I **have** also found over the years that finding the right CPA for you is a very important business decision. I <u>interview CPA's</u> before I hire one. During the interview, I look the applicant dead in the eyes and say:

"I am going to make a lot of money, and I am not planning on paying any taxes."

Now, I know I will have to pay some taxes, but the reaction of the accountant lets me know who I am dealing with. <u>I want to make sure my accountant is going to work hard for me</u>, not just charge me for keeping my records. I also want to make sure the accountant is going to work for me, not the government.

I once had the pleasure of experiencing an Internal Revenue Service audit. The audit revealed that I owed $75,000 to the government in taxes. I never believed I owed that much money, but my CPA told me I had to pay it. I decided to fire the CPA and I was given an extension by the IRS. The same thing happened to my next three accountants.

Two years later, I hired an accountant who knew his business, and he was able to get the amount owed down to three thousand dollars. He then told me what his fee was and I told him I would pay him as soon as he got the amount owed to the IRS down to $0. However, I did not insist that he do this.

Dealing with Banks

I've learned over the years that there is a secret to dealing with banks in order to get a loan. First, you must realize that the banker is not doing you a favor when he decides to lend you money. You are doing him a favor when you borrow money from him.

Start a relationship with the bank you wish to borrow money from at least a year before you need the money. Begin by opening a checking or savings account with the bank manager. Get to know the bank manager very well and each time you make a deposit, take time to shake the manager's hand and let him know you are there.

Keep a good balance in your accounts and don't let any checks bounce. After you have maintained a good balance for the first year ask for a $500 loan even if you don't need it. You have to start building the bank's confidence in your ability to pay them back. If the banker asks you to pledge your savings account against the loan, do not do it. Politely tell the banker you will withdraw your money, and deposit it in a bank that trusts you. Remind them that you have trusted them with your money, they should trust you with their money.

Now the minute your get your loan, take the $500 and deposit it into your savings account and make the required payments on time. After you have paid back the full $500, go to the banker and ask for $1,000. Again, don't spend the money. Deposit it into your savings account and pay it back. This will <u>build your banking relationship</u>.

Choosing an Attorney

Choosing an attorney is another area in which we should apply a lot of wisdom. <u>Make sure the attorney you choose is going to work for you and will take action that will cost you little money</u>. Ask him or her to put in writing what they plan to do before they do anything and especially before you give them a retainer fee.

Attorneys really have a tendency to talk some "good law" or "legal ease" when they are trying to get a retainer fee. And when the trial starts, you would not think this attorney was the same one you paid the retainer to because they seem to have lost the legal ease, that "good law" talk. Also ask for names and telephone numbers of other people they have represented in similar cases.

Once while I was looking for an attorney to handle one of my cases, I went to an attorney who said he required a $3,000 retainer. He said the case would be difficult. I went to another attorney and he handled the case without a retainer and was able to settle out of court for $200, only charging me a $250 fee.

My experience has taught me that you can avoid a lot of litigation if you hear from an attorney by letter before he brings a crazy lawsuit. The way you answer that letter can make you or break you. Listen to this sound advice:

1) Do not write that letter yourself.
2) Get your attorney to answer that letter while you supervise the tone of the letter.
3) When they answer the letter, you and your attorney should look for ways you can go after the attorney who is bringing that crazy lawsuit.

In other words, connect the attorney to the letter and let the letter be hard hitting. Let him know that you will go after him or her if they bring this crazy lawsuit. Please understand, do not write the other attorney a "sugar-coated" letter under any circumstances. You may have to pay a retainer fee if a suit is filed. If you write a sweet letter, you will be sued.

If your attorney does not agree with this approach, you should run like a rabbit because all he wants to do is collect his attorney's fee. <u>Learn from your experiences</u> as I have learned. Figure out ways to prevent loss in your business and trust God to help you to succeed.

A Comedy Show

Every appointment I go on: banks, CPAs, attorneys, buyers, sellers, visitations at hospitals, doctors, etc.; when I enter the office, the home or the hospital my first approach is to get people laughing. I have a conversation with them to <u>get them laughing</u>. You will be surprised at what will happen. If I had a problem when I went in there, when I come out I feel like I didn't even have a problem.

You want to practice this. <u>Practice and practice this again</u>. Let me give you two examples of what I am talking about. I had a lawsuit. I needed an attorney. When I went to the first attorney, I did not have a comedy show with him. I just walked in there and hit him head-on. He hit me head-on too.

Laughter
is a Something
God has Given to
Everyone

"Mr. Brown," he said, "this is going to be a bad case. I am going to need an attorney's fee of $3,000 for me to handle this case. This is a bad one."

I knew exactly what had taken place. I didn't have a comedy show with the man. I didn't get him laughing. I picked up my file and carried it on down about a half block. But this time before I went into this attorney's office I made the decision I was going to approach him with my comedy show.

265

I got the man so tickled he started laughing. Then he looked down at the file laughing.

"Awe, Brown," he said, "there ain't nothing to this. Bring me $200 to court tomorrow. I will settle this one out of court and the attorney's fee will be $200."

You need to practice this. My wife and I went to Emory Hospital just to take a physical. Just a simple physical. I had to go park the car. My wife went in and filled out my information sheet. Boy, she put on there what my mother died with, what my father died with, all my brothers, and my uncles. When I went in, four doctors got around me declaring I had heart trouble.

The only way I could get them off my back was to suggest that they put me on a treadmill. Let me tell you, I was on that treadmill five times. Every time I got on the treadmill, they asked me how I was doing. I would tell them to speed it up. I did it five times.

They took me off the treadmill and carried me back in the office. Now, I have never known my daddy to run around at night but I put this on him.

"If my daddy didn't have no better sense to run around at night," I said to these four doctors, "he should have died with the heart trouble."

I got those guys so tickled I don't even believe they sent me a bill. You know they did though. If you had been passing the
266

door you would have thought, it was a comedy show going on in there. The experiences of my 48 years say, *"If you accept the diagnosis, it is all over."* I even said to those four doctors.

"If God had nerve enough to bring me here, I believe the God I serve has enough nerve to tell me when it is time to go."

Never Accept
a Negative Diagnosis

Awe, you need to practice this. This comedy show, getting people laughing before you present your problems will take you to the stars. I want you to think for a moment. Didn't God give every man and lady on this earth the ability to laugh?

We have everything in the world to work with, but we often just will not use what the Lord has provided; and it stares us right in the face -- laughter and a smile. We prefer going in there with frowns on our faces. If we approach life this way, we are always going to accept what man says and come out a loser.

I'm talking about how to keep the thieves out of your business, "Doing it God's Way". If you will take what I have shared with you in this chapter and put it into practice, the only people who will be able to compete with you are the people that have this knowledge and use it. We must remember, when we start acknowledging to God, speaking to God, asking Him to intervene, we are going to have to do it by the letter. This is serious business. Don't play with this course.

஠   ஊ

.:PAUSE:. Wealth Building Scriptures
Week 14 – My Daily Commitment

1. Sunday – "He sent his word, and healed them, and delivered *them* from their destructions." Psalm 107:20.

2. Monday – "Then I told them of the hand of my God which was good upon me; as also the king's words that he had spoken unto me. And they said, Let us rise up and build. So they strengthened their hands for *this* good *work*." Nehemiah 2:18.

3. Tuesday - "Neither shall thy name any more be called Abram, but thy name shall be Abraham; for a father of many nations have I made thee." Genesis 17:5.

4. Wednesday – "No weapon that is formed against thee shall prosper; and every tongue *that* shall rise against thee in judgment thou shalt condemn. This *is* the heritage of the servants of the LORD, and their righteousness *is* of me, saith the LORD." Isaiah 54:17.

5. Thursday – "And we know that all things work together for good to them that love God, to them who are the called according to *his* purpose." Romans 8:28.

6. Friday – "*They that are delivered* from the noise of archers in the places of drawing water, there shall they rehearse the righteous acts of the LORD, *even* the righteous acts *toward the inhabitants* of his villages in Israel: then shall the people of the LORD go down to the gates." Judges 5:11.

7. Saturday – "This *is* my comfort in my affliction: for thy word hath quickened me." <u>Psalm 119:50</u>; "For the LORD shall be thy confidence, and shall keep thy foot from being taken." <u>Proverb 3:26</u>.

8. Bonus – "A time to weep, and a time to laugh; a time to mourn, and a time to dance;" <u>Ecclesiastes 3:4</u>; "Blessed *are ye* that hunger now: for ye shall be filled. Blessed *are ye* that weep now: for ye shall laugh." <u>Luke 6:21</u>.

9. Bonus – "**A Psalm of David.** The earth *is* the LORD's and the fullness thereof; the world, and they that dwell therein." <u>Psalm 24:1</u>; "Thy word *is* a lamp unto my feet, and a light unto my path." <u>Psalm 119:105</u>.

(Read Wealth Building Scriptures Aloud-3x Daily)

.:PAUSE:. Wealth Building Tips
Week 14 – My Daily Affirmation

1. Sunday – I will prevent loss in my businesses by hiring competent people who have integrity.

2. Monday – I interview accountant professionals before I put them on retainer. Before I hire anyone, I want to make sure he or she is going to work on my behalf.

3. Tuesday – When I go to the bank, I will walk in knowing I have the Promises of Abraham with me. I will get to know the bank manager very well, because I do him a favor when I borrow money.

4. Wednesday – I will make sure the attorney I choose is going to work for me and will take action that will cost me little money.

5. Thursday – I will learn from my experiences and attempt not to repeat the poor ones.

6. Friday – I will practice the attributes of professionalism and integrity as I execute of my daily responsibilities until they become an integral part of me.

7. Saturday – I will never accept a negative diagnosis.

8. Bonus – I will use laughter as a doorknob to the door of opportunity to my personal business success.

9. Bonus – I have everything in me that I need to work towards my personal success.

(Read Wealth Building Tips Aloud-3x Daily)

Chapter 15

See the Vision

Using the
P.A.U.S.E. ®
(Practical Application and Use of the Scriptures Everyday)
Wealth Building System

"Then spake the Lord to Paul in the night by a vision, Be not afraid, but speak, and hold not thy peace:"

Acts 18:9

Doing It God's Way®

Chapter 15

See the Vision

Blood of Jesus Prayer

Now let us talk about using the <u>Blood of Jesus prayer</u>. I wrap five businesses everyday in the Blood of Jesus. I don't care what kind of business it is. If it is in this kingdom and that businessman is serving God's people, I wrap it with the Blood of Jesus. They don't know I'm doing it. I'm trying to please one God and one Jesus; not man. God knows I'm doing it. I'm a businessman. I have had many businesses.

Why shouldn't I wrap the other people's businesses? If it worked for Sam Brown and he was a rich man, it can work for you. I never heard this farmer say he didn't have any money. He sent seven of my sisters and brothers through college. He had four girls in college at the same time and he was just a farmer. He paid his 98-acre farm off in the 29's when everyone else was losing their farms.

I don't know about you, but I want everything that is rightfully mine. But the only way you are going to operate like I operate is to do Christ's program like He did when He walked this earth. <u>We are supposed to be following Christ</u>, the only Son God had. If you do it any other way, it is true, you may fly for a while; but I promise you God sees everything. He hears everything and we cannot fool Him. That quicksand is going to grab you one of these days and you will not know how it happened. Get smart and receive the real promises of God.

I've had people to ask me when I tell them I've been rich three times and I'm on my way back on my fourth trip this

Don't Do the Same Thing All the Time

question, "What did you do with all that money?" It works this way. When we move from level to level, sometimes we are going to go down and come back again. A righteous man will fall seven times before he leaves this earth. I don't know about you, but I do not want to do the same thing all the time.

<u>I want a lot of experiences</u>. You should want a lot of experiences also. Because with more experience you can help more people move in God's direction on their paths. That is the way you live a long life. That is the way you stay here on this earth and help God's people. What good is a lot of success with a short life?

I wrap five businesses with the Blood of Jesus everyday,

276

seven days a week. I wrap five people that have some type of problem, everyday seven days a week. When that person gets well, you will know about it. I drop that one and pick up another one, but I keep five going all the time.

Every time I pass out flyers for this business, I go by the nursing homes and encourage the people. When I go, most of the time I see between 10 or 15 people. I don't even know the people, but when I go my first approach is to get them laughing. I don't go in there praying. I go in there getting them laughing. See when I get them laughing, I get them on track with me.

When We Move Like Jesus God Gives Us Assignments

When I get them on track with me, now I'm ready to pray with them and teach them how to use the Blood of Jesus. I teach them how to do the *Pathway to Success*®. In other words, I talk to them about getting out of the wheelchair. If Christ did it, they can too. I go to get those people out of their wheelchairs and their beds. Those people that are in those situations are God's people too.

Now you might ask, "How do I get God seeing what I do?" Just go out there and start. Just like I did. Go out there and start it just like Sam Brown did. God will start giving you assignments. That is when you are on your way. However, make sure, make sure that you go and do it. Do not even think about satan. The devil is not going to give us anything that is going to bring us into a closer relationship with God. We spend too much time talking about satan. The devil cannot do anymore to you than what God allows.

God owns it all and without Him, you and I cannot do anything. I wrap the church that is tailor-made for me with the Blood of Jesus three times a day. I wrap my church pastor and the first lady everyday with the Blood of Jesus three times a day. I wrap all the members of the church with the Blood of Jesus everyday, three times a day. The choir, I wrap with the Blood of Jesus three times a day. That is the way you go to the "Promised Land".

I wrap the grass in my yard at home. The plants in my home, the plants around my home I wrap with the Blood of Jesus. The lady that did my typing, the lady who does the house cleaning that comes every two weeks, I wrap them with the Blood of Jesus three times.

Every time I hire a person to do something for my family and I, I wrap them with the Blood of Jesus three times a day. My wife had surgery on her eyes. I wrapped the doctors with the Blood of Jesus before performance time.

"The surgery," the doctor said when he walked out of the surgery, "was successful."

You need to know how to do this and it comes from practice, practice, and more practice. You will never do it by just listening to these tapes, playing these CD's, and reading my books one time. This requires concentration, repetition,

278

and believing the concepts. If you question it, if you doubt it, it won't work.

Examples How To Proceed

I'm going to give you some examples of how to wrap people in the Blood of Jesus. Ask God for your assignments, because God will give you assignments and you must go out there and practice. While waiting on your God-given assignments, you will surely see many situations during your days and nights which give you ample opportunity to respond to someone's moment of need. You have got to get it in your bloodstream that you must help when and where you can.

God gave me an assignment when O. J. Simpson went to trial. I had to wrap him everyday that trial existed. When former President Bill Clinton walked into office, I had to wrap him with the Blood of Jesus everyday without missing. You remember when the Atlanta Braves played in the World Series and won it? I had to warp them everyday with the Blood of Jesus. And what about Magic Johnson's HIV/AIDS? I wrapped him too. They may not believe it; and you may not either. I am telling you what I did and the rest is history. There it is.

You need to know how to do this and <u>go out there and practice</u>. Practice in some awesome situations. Let God see you in action. God will start giving you assignments. Start practicing. I wrap five nursing homes with the Blood of Jesus three times a day.

I feel good when I start wrapping a nursing home with the Blood of Jesus. I'm talking about the patients in there. I go in there, look at them then start wrapping them with the Blood three times a day, five days a week. When I go back to see them again, some do not even look like the same people.

<u>You need to practice doing this Blood of Jesus prayer</u>. I am going to give you some examples of how I do it. Before I do this, let me say this to you for what it is worth, I gave up an income of over $300,000 a year for a period of 22 years to prepare this course for you. Use it!

ဆာ   ၊

Atlanta Nursing Homes

Five Atlanta nursing homes are wrapped everyday in the Blood of Jesus, three times a day. God asked me to do this. Let me give you an example.

According to Romans 5:9, by the Blood of Jesus, the Sadie G. Made Nursing and Rehabilitation Center is justified. The Sadie G. Made Nursing and Rehabilitation Center has been made righteous. The Sadie G. Made Nursing and Rehabilitation Center has fellowship with the Father, according to Ephesians 1:7. By the Blood of Jesus, the Sadie G. Made Nursing and Rehabilitation Center is redeemed and brought back out of the authority of any present evil.

According to Ephesians 1:7, all the sins of the Sadie G. Made Nursing and Rehabilitation Center are completely forgiven by the Blood of Jesus. According to 1 John 1:7, the Blood of Jesus Christ, God's Son is now cleansing the Sadie G. Made Nursing and Rehabilitation Center from all sins. 1 Corinthians 6:19:20, all individuals involved with the Sadie G. Made Nursing and Rehabilitation Center are the temples of the Holy Ghost.

The Sadie G. Made Nursing and Rehabilitation Center is righteous, redeemed, and forgiven. The Sadie G. Made Nursing and Rehabilitation Center is cleansed by the Blood of Jesus. Therefore satan has no power over the Sadie G. Made Nursing and Rehabilitation Center. Satan you have no place with the Sadie G. Made Nursing and Rehabilitation Center. The Sadie G. Made Nursing and Rehabilitation Center renounces you satan. They loose themselves from you satan. They cast you out of their lives. Depart satan and leave the

281

Sadie G. Made Nursing and Rehabilitation Center alone. The individuals involved with the Sadie G. Made Nursing and Rehabilitation Center are righteous sons and daughters of God. Amen.

Not only do I wrap five nursing homes everyday seven days a week; I go visit those nursing homes. When I go, I go there to encourage God's people to get them out of their wheelchairs and beds. But my initial approach when I go is to have a comedy show with them. Before I start praying for them, I get them laughing. Once I get them laughing, life takes on a new meaning. They accept me better

> Wrap People
> Places and Things
> in the Blood of Jesus
> Three times a Day

when I have a comedy show with them. Then I hit them head-on praying. I pray with them after I get them laughing.

I wrap five businesses in the Atlanta area everyday with the Blood of Jesus. I wrap them before I wrap my own business with the Blood of Jesus. Moreover, it works the same way I wrapped the Atlanta Braves with the Blood of Jesus. I am a businessperson, why shouldn't I do it.

The way we get God's attention is to become more concerned about His people than we are about ourselves. God knows that you are concerned about people if you spend the time to do this for them. I wrap five people that have some type of problem everyday three times a day. One time for the Father, one time for the Son, and one time for the Holy Spirit.

282

I have to have the strength and the know-how to do God's work and you do too.

Now, how do you get all this in, in a day's work and still do your other work. I know that is running through your mind. It is so simple. When I started it, I didn't start it this way. God sent me to the Mt. Paran Church on Highway 41 in Atlanta, Georgia. Dr. Paul Walker was the pastor at that time. God sent me there one night. When I arrived, Terry Law was speaking. He was from the Law Outreach World Ministries. The address: Law Outreach World Ministries, P. O. Box 3563, Tuscaloosa, Oklahoma, 74101.

> There is a
> Price We Pay
> to Get the Things
> We Want

He was teaching the people how to use this prayer. God sent me there to get this prayer. Not only did he send me there to get this prayer, but he taught me how to use this prayer. He wanted me to incorporate it into this program.

This prayer is powerful. I have seen some fantastic results by using this prayer. I use this prayer even on myself. When my joints or my legs ache, I wrap them with the Blood, just like I did on the Atlanta Braves. Just like I did on former President Bill Clinton. My heart had irregular beats; I wrapped myself with the Blood of Jesus. Unless you believe these concepts it will not work, but it works for me.

Unless you are following Christ, it will not work. If you are just reading your Bible, hearing the Word preached, tithing your money, and giving offerings and you are not out there changing tears into joy, this will not work for you. You are

283

going to have to do everyday that which Christ did when He walked this earth. Then you will get the results that you are looking for. You may be getting the results now that you are looking for, but there is coming a day when what you are doing now is not going to work for you. Then you can apply these procedures.

Awe, you will see a big difference if you believe the concepts from the tip of your head to the bottom of your feet. There will be a difference. I have been to doctors and they have given me several diagnoses. I turn right around and wrap myself with the Blood of Jesus and go back and take the physical again. They do not see the problem anymore. If I can do this, you can too.

Now, I'm going to make a strong suggestion here. Get in on this regardless of who is listening to this tape or reading this book. <u>The way you get God's attention is to become more concerned about His people than you are about yourself</u>. I cannot over-emphasize this.

଼ଡ଼   ଡ଼଼

We Have to
Pay the Price

We can want it all day long, but we are going to have to pay the price for it just like God's only Son paid the price for each one of us. And paying the price is no more than drinking a glass of water, but you will discover like I have, that water will be the best glass of water you have ever tasted.

Now my wife couldn't see me giving up $300,000 a year. She used to talk about selling is a gift. But she doesn't understand, every job I go on, every business I open up, every church I join, I acknowledge to God and He directs my path. If you do it any other way, you are going to have a rough time in this land. Let me quote the Bible to you: "Blessed *is* every one that feareth the LORD; that walketh in his ways. For thou shalt eat the labour of thine hands: happy *shalt* thou *be*, and *it shall be* well with thee. Thy wife *shall be* as a fruitful vine by the sides of thine house: thy children like olive plants round about thy table." (Psalm 128:1-3)

That is the way I operate. My family and I haven't had to want for anything since we have been in this world. *"If you fear Me, I will give you anything you ask of Me."* If you deviate from the law (from what God says), if the wife wants to go east and God says go west; if you are the head of that household, you are in serious trouble if you go the wrong way.

I was in the hospital visiting. A man was lying there on his back; he had cancer on both sides of his neck. I asked him why was he sick.

285

"I know why I am sick," he said. God called me to preach. I loved my wife, then my fiancé. She said she was not going to be married to a preacher."

I just looked at this man and told him point blank that he was going to leave this earth. And I asked him if he had any insurance.

"They are going to cover you up real quick," I told him. "In a few hours that wife is going to be married to someone else and you say you love your wife. What about Jesus Christ? What about God? He said, *'Put no man before Me,'* and that includes the wife."

Do not Deviate from God's Directions

So this man started talking this way. "If I could get out of here," he said, "and go get me a church and start preaching from the pulpit, I will go right now."

"You don't have to do it that way," I said to him. "You can start preaching right from the bed, right now. When the doctors come in, bring them to Christ. Start talking about how good Jesus and God has been to you. You can make that come back right now. You don't have to go get a church building. You don't have to stand up in a pulpit." I continued. "You can make that come back right now. And when the wife comes in to see you, bring her to Christ too."

Start talking about how good God and Jesus has been to you. A whole new universe will open up to you. Believe it from
286

the tip of your head to the bottom of your feet. It might upset the wife a little while, or the husband, or the children, but we are not talking about a little while here, we are talking about eternity. We are talking about bringing her, him or them to Christ and you walking like Christ. *"When two gather together in my name, I'm in the medication. Whatever you ask of Me, I will do it."* Practice the P.A.U.S.E. Wealth Building System's Wealth Building Scriptures and Tips at the end of each chapter and watch your business and personal life bloom.

සා   ඣ

.:PAUSE:. **W**ealth **B**uilding **S**criptures
Week 15 – My Daily Commitment

1. Sunday – "Much more then, being now justified by his blood, we shall be saved from wrath through him. Romans 5:9; Ephesians 1:7; 1 Corinthians 6:19-20, 1 John 1:7.

2. Monday - "For I have given you an example, that ye should do as I have done to you." John 13:15; "For even hereunto were ye called: because Christ also suffered for us, leaving us an example, that ye should follow his steps." 1 Peter 2:21.

3. Tuesday - "In whom we have redemption through his blood, the forgiveness of sins, according to the riches of his grace;" Ephesians 1:7; 1 Corinthians 6:19-20, 1 John 1:7; Romans 5:9.

4. "Trust in the LORD with all thine heart; and lean not unto thine own understanding. In all thy ways acknowledge him, and he shall direct thy paths." Proverbs 3:5-6.

5. Wednesday – "For I was an hungred, and ye gave me meat: I was thirsty, and ye gave me drink: I was a stranger, and ye took me in: naked and ye clothed me: I was sick, and ye visited me: I was in prison, and ye came unto me." Matthew 25:35-36; Matthew 25:31-46.

6. Friday – "What? Know ye not that your body is the temple of the Holy Ghost *which is* in you, which ye have of God, and ye are not your own? For ye are

bought with a price: therefore glorify God in your body, and in your spirit, which are God's." 1 Corinthians 6:19-20; 1 John 1:7; Romans 5:9; Ephesians 1:7.

7. Saturday – "Greater love hath no man than this, that a man lay down his life for his friends." John 15:13.

8. Bonus – "Thine, O LORD, *is* the greatness, and the power, and the glory, and the victory, and the majesty: for all *that is* in the heaven and in the earth *is thine*; thine *is* the kingdom, O LORD, and thou art exalted as head above all." 1 Chronicles 29:11; 1 John 5:4.

9. Bonus - ""Ye shall walk after the LORD your God, and fear him, and keep his commandments, and obey his voice, and ye shall serve him, and cleave unto him." Deuteronomy 13:4; Deuteronomy 11:27; Deuteronomy 27:10; Deuteronomy 30:2,8,20.

(Read Wealth Building Scriptures Aloud-3x Daily)

.:PAUSE:. Wealth Building Tips
Week 15 – My Daily Affirmation

1. Sunday - I will use the Blood of Jesus prayer to help someone today.
2. Monday - I am going to follow the example of Christ Jesus today.
3. Tuesday - I will position my life to have different experiences.
4. Wednesday - I will ask God for my assignments.
5. Thursday - As I live each day, I will practice turning tears into joy.
6. Friday - I will wrap five people who have problems, everyday three times a day with the Blood of Jesus.
7. Saturday - I will get God's attention by being more concerned about His people than I am about myself.
8. Bonus - I know there is a price I must pay for success. I can want success all day long, but I am going to have to pay the price for it by working for it.
9. Bonus - I will not deviate from God's Directions.

(Read Wealth Building Tips Aloud-3x Daily)

Chapter 16

Be the Best

Using the
P.A.U.S.E.®
(Practical Application and Use of the Scriptures Everyday)
Wealth Building System

"This is my commandment, That ye love one another, as I have loved you. Greater love hath no man than this, that a man lay down his life for his friends. Ye are my friends, if ye do whatsoever I command you."

John 15:12-14

Doing It God's Way®

Chapter 16

Be the Best

Get God's Attention

I **asked my daddy** how could he afford to spend all that time with vocational agriculture teachers and county agents from all over the entire state of North Carolina.

"You are not even making a dime out of this," I said to him. "How can you afford to do it?"

I never forgot that concept he said to me. He looked at me, that grin on his face, I never forgot it over my 48-year track record.

"I cannot afford not to help them," he said. "<u>The way you get God's attention is to be more concerned about God's people than you are about yourself.</u>"

I used that concept all the way through my 48-year track record but I haven't been a farmer once—the principles are the same.

I went into several fields and succeeded in every field, making millions. If I can do it this way, you can too. I would see my daddy sit early in the morning around 3:00 a.m. when everyone was sound asleep.

—————————————

Listen for God's Message

—————————————

You got to understand I was up observing him. I used to see him sitting there reading his Bible, but I never did see him turn a page. I asked him why. Tears running down his cheek, like I said, I never did see him turn a page.

Here again he looked at me with that grin on his face, that serious grin.

"A lot of boys," he said, "talk about reading the Bible. I do the *Pathway to Success*®. A lot of material is in that Bible; materials in the Bible that do not fit today's assignment."

Then he shared with me how God directs his path on how to meditate on that Word.

"The first thing you do," he said, "is to take everything out of the Bible--everything. You want to make sure those leaves are turning by God's power and you hold your hands directly under the Bible, both hands, and you say Father in the name of Jesus let your Word open to where you want me to mediate today."

"Sometimes when you are doing this," he said, "the Bible will open to the same two pages for a number of days, every morning without missing. Then again, sometimes you start this program and it will open to the same two pages two mornings in a row; then the following morning, it will move to two different pages. Then you may not see those pages for weeks or months." He continued. "What God is really showing you when you are repeating those chapters," he said, "is you haven't gotten the message yet."

Why jump all through the Bible and you haven't got His Message. The Message is what you want.

"You read it aloud," my daddy said, "reading it aloud will improve your voice. A good voice is a must to make it in this land. And you read it three times."

One time for the Father, one time for the Son, and one time for the Holy Spirit. I have to have the strength and the know-how to do God's Will and you do too.

You start reading from the left and you go to the right. At the beginning of that first chapter to your left, most likely you are going to have to turn a page to complete that chapter or that Psalm. You read that chapter or that Psalm three times before you leave it.

And before you leave that chapter or the Psalm, practice lifting those hands. Lift those hands as high as you can. Get them thanking God for directing your path. Thanking Him for everything He has done for you since you have been in this world. The more you do this, the more blessings will come down to you.

Each morning after you do that Pathway to Success® you are free to read anywhere in the Bible where you want to read,

295

after you do it three times; every morning, seven days a week. One time for the Father, one time for the Son, and one time for the Holy Spirit. You have to have the know-how and the strength to do God's work.

If you will start doing this, a whole new universe will open up to you, but you have got to believe this concept from the tip of your head to the bottom of your feet. While you are reading your Bible, you are going to start getting ideas concerning what to do in life and how to do it. I succeeded in several fields using this concept and made millions in every field.

The Holy Spirit has been my teacher for a period of 48 years. The Holy Spirit wants to be your teacher too. Unless we do it this way, we are going to always wonder where it is. I have been to the "Promised Land" three times and I am on my way back there on my fourth trip. I am a strong 81 years of age and that in itself should be enough to get your attention.

If you just pick up your Bible and read it where you want to read it, remember God is a good God and He is a jealous God. He tells us so clearly, *"If you acknowledge Me, I will direct your paths."*

He knows what you and I need at all times as individuals. If Sam Brown did it and Sam Brown sent seven of my sisters and brothers to college, you can too. And he did it during the Depression years, just like the bad economic times we are experiencing now. He had four girls in college at the same time. He traded new cars every three years, never got loans, always paid cash and he was only a farmer. And like I said, I never heard of this farmer saying he didn't have any money.

That is the way you get that breakthrough. That is the way you go to that next level. Talk about the enemy leaving, start doing your reading in your Bible that way and your enemies will surely flee. When the Holy Spirit wakes me up every morning around 3:00 a.m., it is time for that *Pathway to Success*®.

Some mornings I'm so sleepy and tired I don't want to get up but I've got to go. It is nothing but a habit. Now, it's true you may not finish that reading, but let me say this to you. Try to do it a least half of it, but before 12:00 midnight that same day. Complete that *Pathway to Success* alone, aloud, and listen to the words. The enemy has got to flee because now you are *"Doing it God's Way"*. A whole new universe will open up to you.

පැ   ඬ

U.S. Government Service

When I left college I became an officer in the United States Army. I immediately got orders for Korea. I had just gotten married; a man going to Korea, just out of college. I was stationed at Fort Dix, NJ.

I had orders for Korea. In Korea, a lieutenant was no more than a rabbit during the opening of hunting season. Any lieutenant, African-American or not, at that time was sure to go into combat, heading to the front lines.

I acknowledged to God. This is the way I did it.

"Father in the name of Jesus," I said, "why are you sending me to Korea? You own everything. I acknowledged you Father to find out what I should do about the girlfriend in high school. You told me to leave her behind. I obeyed you Father."

God wants us to talk to him brave. Man to man, woman to woman, or child to child; with courage. <u>Be not afraid</u>.

"I married the woman you told me to marry," I said. "She is teaching in Fayetteville, NC. Now you are sending me to Korea, but you have a base at Fort Bragg, North Carolina. What are you going to do about it Father?"

God, replied. "Write a letter to the Pentagon."

I did it exactly the way God told me to do it. See, if we try to put our two cents worth in there, it is not going to work.

I made the mistake of showing this letter to my commanding officer at Fort Dix, NJ. He ran and got his regulation book. He showed it to me.

"There is no where in this book that says an officer can get off combat duty because he just got married," he said.

> Believe...
> What God Says
> is True

But you don't bring me a message like that. I know what God said. You don't bring it to me, because I'm not going to hear a word you said.

They even put a song together at the Officer's Club at Fort Dix, New Jersey. Five or six officers formed a train, imitating a train saying, *"Old Brown going A-W-O-L, old Lt. Brown going A-W-O-L."*

You don't frighten me.

"Write a letter to the pentagon," that Voice said.

I didn't write it. I got a professional to write it. I told him to write it and make them cry. I mailed that letter. I came home on my 30-day leave. Boy, my uniform was just sparkling. Those silver bars were just sparkling, but Lt. Brown knew he wasn't going to Korea. Everyone was telling me that I was on my way to Korea. Everyone but AC Brown.

People will steal it from you if you let them. They will attempt to steal your future. They will attempt to steal your joy. But you have got to know; and know that you know. I was not going to allow anyone to steal my joy, to steal my expectation, to steal my future, especially when God said how it was to be.

I didn't know it was going to happen in San Francisco. but it did. I flew all the way to San Francisco with a classmate named Johnny Freeman. He graduated with me and got his commission with me. But I told him I was going to separate from him in a few days.

"Brown," he said, "you are crazy."

"No, I'm not crazy," I said, " I know what the Man said."

"Write a letter to the Pentagon."

On a hot day in front of a formation of two thousand officers ready for combat; rifles, steel pots on, ready for battle, here comes a man running across the field with a loudspeaker in his hand.

"Lt. Brown, you are on your way back to Fort Bragg, North Carolina."

Now the boys in their battle fatigues in the ranks sounded like they were saying this in unison to me, "You lucky dog."

I told you it works.

Why talk about faith? Don't just talk about it – act it out. That is the way you go to the "Promised Land". *Faith without works is death*. When I arrived at Fort Bragg, North Carolina I had 15 months left in my commission. I either had to reinstate my enrollment in the Army or give it up. I gave it up.

Do What is Right

Let me introduce you to one of my contractors, Johnny Langston. I placed an ad in the paper to get this man. When I hire someone, I don't just put an ad in the paper and interview people. I don't do it that way. When I put the ad in the paper, describing what I want, I turn right back around when the ad goes in the paper and acknowledge to God. I tell God about the ad, when it's coming out and who to send me. I give God the description of the job.

All you have to do is keep your mind on God and watch for the man or woman you are going to hire. In 24 hours, I will know spiritually whether he or she is God's man or God's woman. Boy this brother, Johnny Langston was so heavy in the building business that he could figure building materials so close he could put the leftovers in the trunk of his automobile. I interviewed only one man. I put him on the job. These people like Johnny who come to you haven't been to any big-time school but they are pros at what they do.

There is another world of people out there who are educated through experience. I don't know about you but I have been through a thousand storms and have learned from each one. Take advantage of your storms because you may see them again in some form or fashion.

301

Johnny was the type of Caucasian brother who would come by my office in the afternoon and address me this way.

"Mr. Brown is there anything else you want me to do for you before I retire for the afternoon?"

I could leave Johnny in charge running several crews. I could leave him in charge running that construction company for 60 days or 90 days without me even showing up. Awe, you can go places with a man like that. Johnny developed several subdivisions and built thousands of homes for me.

We built the Brown Construction Company office building directly across the street of A&T College; directly across the street of the same college where I made those C's and D's. When I used to drive up to the Brown Construction Company office building, I would look over and wave my transcript at them while I made millions. Let me make an observation here.

God Will See Us Through Any Storm

I am not de-emphasizing striving to make good grades in school. <u>I am emphasizing that you take what you have regardless of what it is and go into the land, finding a need that needs filling</u>. Then you acknowledge God (keep God involved in your plans) and let Him direct your path and teach you how to fill that need. I don't care if it rains down fire, snow, hail, and sleet. You stay on the drawing board until it happens. That is the way you create wealth and increase your wealth. You know what is right and wrong. <u>Just do it right and God will see you through the storm</u>.

Let God Direct Your Path

I **joined** the Home Builders Association in Greensboro, NC. How did that come about? One morning I was in my *Pathway to Success*® class with God, His Son, and the Holy Spirit. I heard that voice.

"Join the Home Builders Association in Greensboro, North Carolina".

I joined the North Carolina Home Builders Association. I was the only African-American in the organization. Now, I was competing with all the other contractors in Greensboro in my home building price range for business opportunities. Then I

entered the "Parade of Homes" contest in North Carolina where hundreds of Caucasian brothers were competing for top honors. Some of those Caucasian brothers were building thousands of homes on a yearly basis. But remember this always, <u>through God, all things are possible for him that believes</u>. Now I was in competition with some strong competitors. I was prepared but I continued my preparation because I wanted to be the best.

In the year of 1965, Brown Construction Company and Real Estate Company won the "Parade of Homes." Thousands of people from all over the entire state of North Carolina toured the home which the Brown Construction Company built. And guess who drew the plans? My wife, Gladys Lea Ruffin Brown.

In fact, Lea Ruffin Brown drew all the plans that the Brown Construction and Real Estate Company built -- and drew plot plans for the subdivision. Now, I don't know what the girl who God said to leave behind back there in high school could have done, but that's none of my business, that's God's business.

The God I serve directs my path and the only reason He is directing my path is I acknowledge Him. <u>You have got to develop the habit of acknowledging Him in everything you do in life.</u> He tells you so clearly, *"If you acknowledge Me, I will direct your path."* Don't play with it unless you mean business. He told me to leave that girl in high school behind and I did. He knew why. I did not.

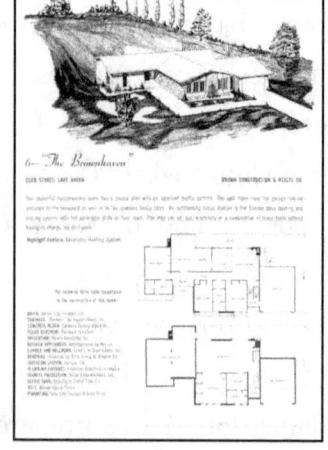

God knows what He is doing. If you are just reading the Bible and are not understanding what to do in life's situations and you need what I am sharing with you to effectively handle, through God, your challenges, <u>read this book daily. Do "Your Daily Affirmations" and "Your Daily Commitment."</u> Do them daily, three times a day. Over and

304

over, and over again, remembering that repetition is a wonderful thing. Then go out there and do it the way Christ did it—turn tears into joy.

Play the audiotapes and CD's over and over again so the information will "stick." Along with that, <u>go out there and apply what you have learned</u>.

Let Go

What We Need

To Let Go

Apply it again and again. Do it, and do it and do it again. <u>As long as you just sit, and sit and sit and read, and read and read and don't try it and attempt it and attempt it again; you will never, never, never ever get the wealth which the Lord has promised you</u>".

Awe, you will be surprised at what will happen when you just try it. It works. You will be surprised. You can talk about it until dooms-day, but if you don't do it, you will never get it going.

I knew a lady who paid $3,000 to take a course and invest in the Real Estate business. She is still driving a bus; afraid to turn that bus loose. <u>You have got to turn that old thing loose, so you can receive that new thing</u>. We can't put something new in our hands when we are holding on to that old thing. <u>Don't worry about failing</u>. God said, *"if you acknowledge to Me, I will direct your path."*

He means it and you must do that *Pathway to Success®* everyday just like I teach you. You will miss the whole mark if you don't. You can be in Revelation reading it because you

305

want to go there and God wants you to be in the Psalms reading there. You will have missed it. This is how not to miss it. You can tell when you are getting ready to be delivered or get your answer. You will be reading Psalms, for instance and it will be talking about "falling." Who is falling? Your enemies are falling. Why are they falling? They are falling because you are doing that *Pathway to Success*® on them. <u>The Scriptures which you are reading is telling God what to do to your enemies; and telling you what God is doing or going to do to your enemies and in your life's situations</u>. That is the way you get the breakthrough. That is the way you do it. There is no guesswork. There is no need to get angry. <u>If you get angry, the only person you are going to mess up is yourself.</u>

℘   ℘

Listen for God Speaking

I got tired of building houses. I wanted to be a Real Estate salesperson. I was at my highest peak as a builder. Here again, I acknowledged to God and He directed my path. I acknowledged to God that I wanted to be a Real Estate salesperson and that I was at my highest peak as a builder. Guess what happened? In 30 days, the building business was over for AC Brown. You have got to do what you said you were going to do for God. It was all over. All the banks that I was borrowing money from called me in and said they were not loaning me another dime.

When you acknowledge God, speak to God, you can't deviate from the plan. If you deviate from the plan, what you are doing is all over. I was walking around Greensboro, NC like a dead man. I didn't know what was wrong. I had one lawsuit I had to deal with before I left Greensboro; one lawsuit. Here again, I acknowledged God to find out where I could get an attorney to handle this case.

God sent me to attorney J. Kenneth Lee. I had never used attorney J. Kenneth Lee before. The whole time I was in Greensboro, NC building houses, the reason I hadn't used him was because my brother-in-law, Bruce Ruffin told me that he was crooked.

"The reason I hadn't used you," I said to attorney J. Kenneth Lee, "is because Bruce, my brother-in-law said you were crooked." I continued. "But the truth of the matter is, I've got to have an attorney. I have a terrible lawsuit and I have to have a good lawyer on this case and God directed me to come to you."

He looked at me and grinned. He said, "Brown, I will represent you."

"Now I don't have the money," I said.

"Just pay me," he said, "when you get it."

How many attorneys do you know who would say, *"Pay me when you get it?"* But when God sends you to a man, please go. God knows exactly what you need. And my experiences

307

have been this way in life for 48 years. When God sends you to a man or lady, He is going to send you to the best in the business.

Attorney J. Kenneth Lee represented me like I had a million dollars in my pocket. Boy, he won that lawsuit. I was driving him back to his office. He rode with me that morning to court. Traveling back to his office, I asked him a question, a serious question. He was reading his book. He answered the question and never did take his head out of the book.

Bring God's Name into Our Everyday Conversation

He dropped the answer the morning after he won the lawsuit. The lawsuit was worth more than a million dollars to me.

"Brown," he said, "you are ready to make you some real money now." He continued. "A lot of people would give their left arm to know what you know."

Then he suggested that I go to Atlanta, Georgia.

That wasn't J. Kenneth Lee talking. That was the Creator. He was sending me a message through attorney J. Kenneth Lee. *If you acknowledge Me, I will direct your path*. I'm going to say this for what it's worth, I don't care to whom you are talking, <u>do not be afraid to bring the name God into the picture</u>. If you don't do it that way, you will always wonder where everything is; nothing will go right for you. The 24th Psalms says it so clearly; *God owns it all* and without Him you and I cannot do anything.

At this point, I want you to stop what you are doing. I want you to just sit there. Don't say a word. Just think about the problems that are worrying you. Think about the little ones and the big ones; the problems in your home and on your job. Now, I want you to spend a few moments where you are sitting and begin laughing. Laughing at those problems. Come on, let's do it. Laugh! Laugh out loud! You are laughing because you have the victory. <u>Claim your victory praising in laughter</u>.

Let me make an observation here. We don't like to talk about God and Jesus in business situations. But I'm going to say this to you for what it's worth, as long as you keep your mouth closed about God and Jesus, you will never get the real promises of God. *<u>If we do not confess Him before men, He will not confess us before our Father who is in Heaven</u>*.

So if we keep on keeping those mouths closed, we are playing with our lives. And the Bible tells us so clearly, *the harvest is plentiful. God owns it all.* God hears everything we say; we can't fool Him. He even knows how we think about this course right now. He knows if you want it or if you don't want it. That power belongs to God. Make the right choices today.

When riches increase, set not your heart pumping. The way we get God's attention, to get God to work on our behalves, <u>we</u>

must become more concerned about God's people than we are about ourselves. Then the promises of God will drop on us and our households just like snowflakes falling from the winter sky.

If you will do it the way I teach you, no man on earth can compete with you. I don't care what kind of field you want to go into; wealth will be yours.

.:PAUSE:. Wealth Building Scriptures
Week 16 – My Daily Commitment

1. Sunday – "And the second *is* like unto it, Thou shalt love thy neighbor as thyself." <u>Matthew 22:39</u>; "But I say unto you, Love your enemies, bless them that curse you, do good to them that hate you, and pray for them which despitefully use you, and persecute you;" <u>Matthew 5:44</u>; <u>Genesis 4:9</u>; <u>Luke 6:27</u>.

2. Monday – "This book of the law shall not depart out of thy mouth; but thou shalt meditate therein day and night, that thou mayest observe to do according to all that is written therein: for then thou shalt make thy way prosperous, and then thou shalt have good success." <u>Joshua 1:8</u>; <u>Proverbs 3:5-6</u>.

3. Tuesday – "Thus will I bless thee while I live: I will lift up my hands in thy name. My soul shall be satisfied as with marrow and fatness; and my mouth shall praise thee with joyful lips:" <u>Psalms 63:4-5</u>; <u>Exodus 29:24</u>.

4. Wednesday – "But the Comforter, *which is* the Holy Ghost, whom the Father will send in my name, he shall teach you all things, and bring all things to your remembrance, whatsoever I have said unto you." <u>John 14:26</u>; <u>Luke 12:12</u>.

5. Thursday – "The blessing of the LORD, it maketh rich, and he addeth no sorrow with it." <u>Proverb 10:22</u>; <u>Malachi 3:10</u>.

6. Friday – "And thou shalt love the Lord thy God with all thy heart, and with all thy soul, and with all thy mind, and with all thy strength: this *is* the first

commandment." <u>Mark 12:30</u>; "*A Psalm* of David. The LORD *is* my light and my salvation; whom shall I fear? The LORD *is* the strength of my life; of whom shall I be afraid?" <u>Psalm 27:1</u>.

7. Saturday – "My mouth shall speak of wisdom; and the meditation of my heart *shall be* of understanding." <u>Psalm 49:3</u>; <u>Psalm 90:12</u>; <u>Psalm 111:10</u>; <u>Proverbs 1:2-5</u>.

8. Bonus – "My brethren, count it all joy when ye fall into divers temptations;" <u>James 1:4</u>; "Be glad in the LORD, and rejoice, ye righteous: and shout for joy, all ye that are upright in heart." <u>Psalm 32:11</u>; <u>Psalm 5:11</u>.

9. Bonus – "Yea, a man may say, Thou hast faith, and I have works: shew me thy faith without thy works, and I will shew thee my faith by my works.: <u>James 2:18</u>; <u>James 2:20, 26</u>, <u>Habakkuk 2:2</u>.

10. Bonus – "For I was an hungred, and ye gave me meat: I was thirsty, and ye gave me drink: I was a stranger, and ye took me in: naked and ye clothed me: I was sick, and ye visited me: I was in prison, and ye came unto me." <u>Matthew 25:35-36</u>; <u>Matthew 25:31-46</u>.

11. "Then shall he answer them, saying, Verily I say unto you, Inasmuch as ye did *it* not to one of the least of these, ye did *it* not to me." <u>Matthew 25:45</u>; <u>Matthew 25:31-46</u>.

(Read Wealth Building Scriptures Aloud-3x Daily)

.:PAUSE:. Wealth Building Tips
Week 16 – My Daily Affirmation

1. Sunday - To get God's attention, I will be more concerned about God's people than I am about myself.

2. Monday - I will do the *Pathway to Success*® daily to get ideas about what to do in life and how to do it.

3. Tuesday - I will lift my hands high when praising God, thanking God for everything He has done for me since I have been in this world.

4. Wednesday - I want the Holy Spirit to be my teacher. I will ask God about each major decision, asking Him to let the Holy Spirit be my Teacher on the assignment.

5. Thursday - I will always have the money that I need.

6. Friday - I will revere God and not be afraid of anything.

7. Saturday - I know what I know; and I know that I know what I know.

8. Bonus - I will not allow anyone to steal my joy, to steal my expectations, or to steal my future.

9. Bonus – I will not only talk about my goals, I will act them out. I realize faith without works is failure.

10. Bonus – Today, I will go into the land and I find a need that needs filling and fill it.

(Read Wealth Building Tips Aloud-3x Daily)

EPILOGUE

How to Use This Book

In **summary,** each book in the Wealth Building series is designed using stories, anecdotes, and biographical information summarizing Alonza C. Brown's life wherein he earned nearly one million dollars three times. Found within the pages of each chapter are the <u>scriptures</u> which he applied throughout his life and the situations to which he applied them. They are <u>underlined</u> within each chapter along with key wealth building <u>tips</u>.

There is a summary of key wealth building scriptures found at the end of each chapter. These "<u>Wealth Building Scriptures</u>" are located in front of the "Wealth Building Tips" also found at the end of each chapter. The "Wealth Building Scriptures" chapter summary, is entitled "<u>My Daily Commitment</u>." You read these scriptures aloud three times a day; good times are at mealtime and at bedtime.

Most of the underlined key wealth building issues are <u>summarized</u> at the end of each chapter in "<u>Wealth Building Tips</u>." The "Wealth Building Tips" chapter summary, is entitled "<u>My Daily Affirmations</u>." These you do three times a day; at mealtime and bedtime is okay.

Each chapter represents a week, i.e., chapter one equals week one. You will notice that the chapter summaries are noted as" "Week One, Week Two, Week Three," and so forth. There are sixteen chapters in this book. This correlates to sixteen weeks. This is a sixteen-week program where success is guaranteed.

This book can be used in your personal home study, your weekly Bible study, or in any weekly or scheduled class which seeks to economically empower its participants. This is an individual or group-- daily, weekly, or sixteen-week program depending on how you want to use it. Use it to compliment your current delivery module.

In summary, Dr. A.C. Brown's P.A.U.S.E. Wealth Building System: Practical Application and Use of Scriptures Everyday is designed based on the life of Alonza C. Brown. He is a three-time millionaire who is imparting into you his secrets of success. This wealth building program has seven cornerstone "wealth building" scriptures and a plethora of "wealth building" tips and information which when applied daily is guaranteed to bring success. These are underlined throughout each chapter.

As you start your day, read each scripture, "My Daily Commitment" (Wealth Building Scripture) aloud three times during the course of a 24-hour period. There is at least one scripture and one tip for each day of the week.

Each chapter will have at least seven scriptures and tips, with bonus scriptures and tips found at the end of some chapters. Say aloud each "My Daily Affirmation" (Wealth Building Tips) three times a day during a 24-hour period.

Do this with each chapter's "Wealth Building Scriptures" and "Wealth Building Tips" for a period of sixteen weeks. You are guaranteed to become a more positive individual, have more success in business and develop better relationships. It works!

Eleanor Thought She Had Security

Eleanor had a good job with a good salary and full benefits. One day I asked Eleanor, "Why don't you learn the business of selling?"

I wasn't criticizing her for her type of employment, but encouraging her to learn the business of selling. Why? Because I have been dealing with the business world for 48 years and I have never heard of a good salesperson getting laid off.

Eleanor replied, "AC, I am doing all right. I have a good job at the data processing company. I get sick leave, vacation pay and I'm working on my retirement fund. Furthermore, my supervisor can't get along without me."

A few weeks ago, my wife and I spent the weekend at her home. That Monday morning we watched Eleanor send her kids off to school. I noticed that she was not rushing off to work. Thinking she had the day off, I asked her.

"Eleanor, how many vacation days are you getting this year?"

As she stood over the stove with her back to me, there was complete silence.

Finally, as she turned around, I noticed her eyes were filled with tears.

She said, "AC I've been laid off. I don't know what I'm going to do. I got my last check on Friday. I haven't even told the children yet. This is Frankie's last year in high school and he has big plans for college next year. My mortgage payment is due the first of the month and the car payment is due on the 10th. How could they do this to me?"

By this time, tears were really flowing. She ended with, "I've been on that job for twelve years".

Suddenly, I was not hungry anymore. I got up from the table and put my arms around her as I tried to find words to console her. I was so choked up that I couldn't say much. While driving back home, I wondered about "the sick leave, the vacation with pay, and the supervisor who couldn't do without her".

What about her mortgage payment and car payment? What about Frankie's college plans? I thought if Eleanor had only taken time out to learn the business of selling while she had that job the day the supervisor brought her that last check. She could have said to him, *"I have nothing to fear because I have prepared myself by learning the business of selling."*

DON'T LET THIS HAPPEN TO YOU!

What if Eleanor had just taken time, while she had that good job, to learn how to sell, that day when the supervisor brought her that last check, all she would have had to do is say mentally, *"I have nothing to fear, because I have prepared myself and everyone in my household have prepared themselves and we know how to sell."*

Now after reading this book, every one of us knows how to acknowledge God and let God direct our paths so we can accomplish everything we want to accomplish in life "Doing it God's Way".

ഓ   ര

**TAKE WHAT GOD GAVE YOU
FROM BIRTH**

**TAKE WHAT YOU OPEN YOUR
MOUTH AND ASK GOD FOR**

HOOK THE TWO TOGETHER

GET PERSONAL SUCCESS

ജ   ര

"Let every thing that hath breath
praise the LORD. Praise ye the LORD."
Psalm 150:6

ജ   ര

NOTES

NOTES

Do not be afraid to try something new. I dare you to do it...

...<u>It works</u>, but you <u>must</u> put in the effort!

www.ingramcontent.com/pod-product-compliance
Lightning Source LLC
Chambersburg PA
CBHW071357170526
45165CB00001B/84